Witnessing, Soul Winning and Discipling

Dr. Jose A. Lagud

©Copyright 1993— Dr. Jose A. Lagud

All rights reserved. This book is protected under the copyright laws of the United States of America. This book may not be copied or reprinted for commercial gain or profit. Short quotations or occasional page copying for personal or group study is permitted and encouraged. Permission will be granted upon request.

Take note that the name satan and related names are not capitalized. We choose not to acknowledge him, even to the point of violating grammatical rules.

Note: All Scripture quotations are taken from the King James Version, unless otherwise indicated as (TLB) The Living Bible; (NIV) New International Version; (NKJ) New King James Version; (RSV) Revised Standard Version; and (NAS) New American Standard Version.

Companion Press
P.O. Box 310
Shippensburg, PA 17257-0310

"Good Stewards of the
Manifold Grace of God"

ISBN 1-56043-540-2

For Worldwide Distribution
Printed in the U.S.A.

Dedicated
to
my loving and understanding
wife Annie, son Joel and daughter Jo-Ann

Contents

Chapter		Page
	Introduction	vii
Part One: Witnessing		1
I	The Importance of Witnessing	3
II	The Believer's Task	9
Part Two: Soul Winning		13
III	The Importance of Soul Winning	15
IV	The Soul Winner's Task	21
V	Qualifications of the Soul Winner	29
VI	Methods of Soul Winning	51
VII	The Approach	59
VIII	Soul Winning Procedure	65

| IX | Dealing With the Prospects .... 79 |
| X | Dealing With the Prospects in General....103 |

Part Three: Discipling 115

| XI | Discipling the New Believer to Spiritual Maturity ....117 |

Appendix A:
Dealing With Prospeccts Who Are
Roman Catholics (Romano Catolico)........141

Appendix B:
Dealing With Prospects Who Are of the
Philippine Independent Church 151

Appendix C:
Dealing With Prospects Who Are of the
Church of Jesus Christ of the Latter Day
Saints..153

Appendix D:
Dealing With Prospects Who Are of the
Seventh Day Adventist Church...................165

Appendix E:
Dealing With Prospects Who Are
Jehovah's Witnesses 179

Appendix F:
Dealing With Prospects Who Are of the
Iglesia ni Cristo (Manalo)............................197

About the Author..225

Bibliography..227

Introduction

This book has been designed in plain and simple words, to help lost souls who read this book to find Jesus Christ as their personal divine Lord and Savior; to encourage and inspire every true born again Christian or true believer to boldly witness for Jesus Christ; to instruct and train the true believer to win and to lead the lost souls to Jesus Christ, that they too may experience the joy of His salvation; and to inspire, guide and equip the soul winner, evangelist and Bible teacher to disciple the new believer or young in faith, that they too may grow to spiritual maturity in the manifold grace and knowledge of God our Father, of Jesus Christ the Son, our Lord and Savior, and of the Holy Spirit, our Guide and our Comforter.

Those faithful servants of the Lord, whether they are witnessing, soul winning or discipling, are all likened to the sowers and reapers who rejoiced together when the fruit is gathered to eternal life.

The Lord assured His servants that there would be great and infinite rewards. If we can be used by the Lord God to bring the lost souls to a saving knowledge of Jesus Christ, it will be the greatest service we can ever render to our fellow man. The Bible says: "And he that reapeth receiveth wages, and gathereth fruit unto life eternal: that both he that soweth and he that reapeth may rejoice together" (John 4:36).

It is my fervent prayer that, by lovingly sharing the truth about salvation, all might see the light and heartily believe and receive Jesus Christ as their personal divine Lord and Savior. That is the only assurance we have of spending eternity with God in a "new heaven and a new earth" (Rev. 21:1), where there will be "no more death, neither sorrow, nor crying, neither shall there be any more pain: for the former things are passed away" (Rev. 21:4).

Part One

Witnessing

Jesus Christ exhorted His disciples to testify for Him. He said; "But ye shall receive power, after that the Holy Ghost is come upon you: and ye shall be witnesses unto Me...unto the uttermost part of the earth" (Acts 1:8).

The word *witness*, according to the dictionary, means "An attesting of facts, statement, etc. evidence; testimony; a person who saw or can give a firsthand account of something" (*Webster New World Dictionary*, 1970).

The Bible says: "For thou shalt be His witness unto all men of what thou hast seen and heard" (Acts 22:15). Witnessing for Jesus Christ, therefore, means that the true believer or the true born again Christian tells the unbeliever or the lost soul what he himself has seen, heard and experienced about Jesus Christ. If he states his opinion about Jesus Christ, he is not witnessing. That type of testimony would not be accepted in a court of law. A witness can only state what he has seen, heard and experienced.

Therefore, every true believer in Jesus Christ or every truly born again Christian, whether only a mere believer, a soul winner, a Bible teacher, an evangelist or a pastor, can testify or witness for Jesus Christ without any preparation. Just tell the lost soul what you have seen, heard and experienced; the things God has done in your life. The Bible says:

That which was from the beginning, which we have heard, which we have seen with our eyes, which we have looked upon, and our hands have handled, of the Word of life;

(For the life was manifested, and we have seen it, and bear witness, and shew unto you that eternal life, which was with the Father, and was manifested unto us;)

That which we have seen and heard declare we unto you, that ye also may have fellowship with us: and truly our fellowship is with the Father, and with His Son Jesus Christ. (I John 1:1-3)

Of course, true believers in Jesus Christ need to pray to God that the Holy Spirit would help, lead and guide them; for without Him they cannot do anything. That is the only preparation they need for the boldness to witness for Jesus Christ, their Lord and Savior.

Chapter I

The Importance of Witnessing

Every True Believer Is to Witness

Every true believer or born again Christian is to witness for Jesus Christ. He commanded His followers to witness for Him. He said: "And ye shall be witnesses unto Me...unto the uttermost part of the earth" (Acts 1:8b).

Every true believer must exert every effort to heed Jesus' command to witness for Him. It is an honor and a privilege to exert effort to witness for Jesus Christ.

Immediately after his conversion, Paul went out witnessing for Jesus Christ. The Bible says:

Instantly (it was as though scales fell from his eyes) Paul could see, and was immediately baptized.

Then he ate and was strengthened. He stayed with the believers in Damascus for a few days

and went at once to the synagogue to tell everyone there the Good News about Jesus—that He is indeed the Son of God! (Acts 9:18-20 TLB)

It was Paul's highest honor and his greatest privilege to witness for Jesus Christ before the audience of a great crowd, before kings and emperors, and even while in prison. In his testimony, he states what Jesus Christ and Ananias told him. He said:

And one Ananias, a devout man according to the law, having a good report of all the Jews which dwelt there,

Came unto me, and stood, and said unto me, Brother Saul, receive thy sight. And the same hour I looked up upon him.

And he said, The God of our fathers hath chosen thee, that thou shouldest know His will, and see that Just One, and shouldest hear the voice of His mouth.

For thou shalt be His witness unto all men of what thou hast seen and heard. (Acts 22:12-15)

Peter and John boldly witnessed for Jesus Christ. When they were told not to speak and teach again in the name of Jesus Christ, they defied the order. They continued to witness for Jesus Christ, telling the things they had seen and heard. The Bible says:

But Peter and John answered and said unto them, Whether it be right in the sight of God to hearken unto you more than unto God, judge ye.

The Importance of Witnessing

For we cannot but speak the things which we have seen and heard. (Acts 4:19,20)

Although Paul did not use the word *privilege* in his letter to the Ephesians (3:1-13), it was the central thought of his epistle. He viewed the true believers or born again Christians as extremely privileged people.

Paul often spoke about his experience with the Lord Jesus Christ on his way to Damascus. He had the experience of physically seeing and talking with the risen Lord. Paul considered his experience with Jesus Christ to be the greatest experience every believer ever had. It was the transformation of his life. Having an experience with the Lord Jesus Christ means a change of life. One has the privilege of turning his life around from the old life to a new life with Jesus Christ (Acts 9:3-18).

Believers Must Have a Part in Jesus' Sufferings

When Paul started witnessing for Jesus Christ, the people who used to praise him for his beliefs in the Jewish religion became his greatest enemies. He encountered the greatest persecution in his life. In fact, they wanted to kill him (Acts 9:23-31).

After his experience with the Lord Jesus Christ, he gave his life to the service of the Lord and called himself "the least of all saints" (Eph. 3:8).

In like manner, when a Christian goes out witnessing for Jesus Christ, he will encounter opposition. He will be ridiculed by the same people who used to praise him and fellowship with him before his conversion.

Carnal Christians are afraid to witness for Jesus Christ; they are scared of being ridiculed and persecuted. But what does the Bible say about the fear of man? It says: "The fear of man bringeth a snare: but whoso putteth his trust in the Lord shall be safe" (Prov. 29:25).

Jesus Christ cautioned His followers not to fear those who could destroy their bodies, but to fear Him who has the power to cast one into hell. Jesus Christ says:

> *And I say unto you My friends, Be not afraid of them that kill the body, and after that have no more that they can do.*
>
> *But I will forwarn you whom ye shall fear: Fear Him, which after He hath killed hath power to cast into hell; yea, I say unto you, Fear Him.* (Luke 12:4,5)

Peter and John, while witnessing for Jesus Christ, were put into prison. Before they were released, they were beaten and commanded not to speak again in Jesus' name. But that just encouraged them to witness more and more for Jesus Christ. They rejoiced that God had counted them worthy to suffer dishonor for Jesus Christ (Acts 5:40-42).

Suffering in Jesus' name is a great honor and privilege. Those who are persecuted because they witness for Jesus Christ are happy. They are happy because their rewards are waiting for them in Heaven. Jesus said:

> *Blessed are they which are persecuted for righteousness' sake: for theirs is the kingdom of heaven.*

The Importance of Witnessing

Blessed are ye, when men shall revile you, and persecute you, and shall say all manner of evil against you falsely, for My sake.

Rejoice, and be exceeding glad: for great is your reward in heaven: for so persecuted they the prophets which were before you. (Matt. 5:10-12)

There are future rewards if we suffer with Him. Not only do we inherit the Kingdom of Heaven and receive great reward, we also are to reign with Him. The Bible says:

It is a faithful saying: For if we be dead with Him, we shall also live with Him:

If we suffer, we shall also reign with Him: if we deny Him, He also will deny us. (II Tim. 2:11,12)

Therefore, every true believer or true born again Christian must witness for Jesus Christ, and even suffer and die with Him if necessary, in order to live and reign with Him.

Chapter II

The Believer's Task

Witnessing Needs No Preparation

Witnessing for Jesus Christ needs no preparation; only the commitment, confidence, compassion and concern to do it. Just pray to God for the Holy Spirit to give you the courage to tell the lost soul the wonderful things God has done for you and the boldness to tell the things you have seen, heard and experienced with the Lord and Savior Jesus Christ.

A new convert can immediately witness for Jesus Christ to any lost soul, at any time and in any place. However, you need to invite that convert to go to church with you. Remember, you must sit with them and guide them, showing them how to find the hymns and the Scripture lessons. The following are some examples of people immediately witnessing.

1. Andrew. When he found Jesus Christ as his Lord and Savior, he immediately witnessed to his brother Simon (called Peter) and introduced him to Jesus Christ, who was teaching. The Bible says:

One of the two which heard John speak, and followed Him, was Andrew, Simon Peter's brother.

He first findeth his own brother Simon, and saith unto him, We have found the Messias, which is, being interpreted, the Christ.

And he brought him to Jesus. And when Jesus beheld him, He said, Thou art Simon the son of Jona: thou shalt be called Cephas, which is by interpretation, A stone. (John 1:40-42)

2. Philip. When he found Jesus Christ, he too was converted. After his conversion, he witnessed to Nathanael. Philip then invited Nathanael to where Jesus Christ was teaching. So Nathanael too was converted (John 1:43-50).

3. The Samaritan woman. After her conversion, she went back to the village and witnessed to the village men and invited them to Jesus Christ by the well. They too became converted (John 4:25-30,39).

4. Paul, who was formerly named Saul. When he was converted, he witnessed where he was at Damascus and those who heard him were amazed (Acts 9:17-21).

5. The man possessed by the demon. When he was converted, he wanted to follow Jesus Christ in order to serve Him. The man pleaded with Jesus Christ to let

him go along with Him, but Jesus said no. Instead, He instructed the man to go home to his friends and tell them the wonderful things the Lord had done for him. The man complied with Jesus' command, and the people who heard him were amazed (Mark 5:18-20).

Where to Start Witnessing

From the examples we just finished looking at, we can see that in witnessing, the first priority is our family, the second is our relatives, and the third is our friends and others.

Also, from those examples, we find several places to begin in witnessing. They include the following:

1. Start witnessing at home to your family. Andrew did it. He witnessed to his brother first. It will be difficult to witness to others if you cannot witness to your own family.

2. Start witnessing for Jesus Christ to relatives, friends and acquaintances from your hometown like the Samaritan woman did. She invited the whole town to meet Jesus Christ by the well.

3. Start witnessing for Jesus Christ to your friends while on your way home like the man possessed by the demon did. Immediately following his conversion, he witnessed to anyone and everyone on his way home.

4. Start witnessing in the place you found Jesus Christ as your personal Lord and Savior. After Paul's conversion in Damascus, he started witnessing right where he was miraculously transformed.

Every true believer can witness anywhere, any time, when opportunity is at hand. Witness to people and invite them to church with you, then introduce them to the trained soul winners, Bible teachers or pastors so the more experienced believer can win them to Jesus Christ, making Him their personal Lord and Savior.

Witnessing is one of the foundations from which a church will grow. If the members refuse to participate in witnessing and soul winning, then there will never be a growth in numbers. But when every member of the church participates, progress is in sight and the church will continue to grow, physically and spiritually.

Part Two

Soul Winning

Jesus Christ set the pattern for winning lost souls. He trained His first converts to become soul winners, teachers and pastors. After their training, He sent them out two by two to win the lost souls. Most of Jesus' converts became witnesses. Some of Jesus' converts became soul winners, teachers and pastors. Almost every convert was involved in His program to save the world from sin.

Before going further, let me define the phrase *soul winning* to set the boundaries and distinctions between soul winning and witnessing. To some these terms are synonymous, or have the same meaning. They are not the same. Soul winning is the act of the trained believer to win and lead the lost soul into believing in Christ Jesus as his personal Lord and Savior in order that he too may experience the joy of His salvation.

From this definition, then, only the trained soul winners, teachers or pastors can successfully accomplish the task of winning the lost souls, with the help and guidance of the Holy Spirit who can convict and convert lost souls.

If we have the gift of winning souls, then we can train ourselves in different ways and develop that gift for the glory of God and for the honor of His Church.

Chapter III

The Importance of Soul Winning

It is the highest honor and the greatest privilege of every trained true believer to be able to help in the building of the Kingdom of God through soul winning. The trained born again Christian who found Jesus as his personal divine Lord and Savior needs to share that experience with others so they too may taste the joy of His salvation.

The Love of God

The love of God is not limited to only a select group of religious people; rather, it embraces the whole human race. The Bible says: "For God so loved the world, that He gave His only begotten Son, that whosoever believeth in Him should not perish, but have everlasting life" (John 3:16). Someone has said: "The entire Gospel of Jesus Christ is summed up in this verse. The deepness of God's love, and the greatness of His gift, and the blessings which He freely gave us is revealed every time we read this verse."

God loved us. That is the reason He sent His only Son; that the lost souls might have everlasting life. Although He loves us all, He has given us the freedom to choose between right and wrong, between Heaven and hell. He would not force us to accept His gift: Jesus Christ. The purpose of His coming is to find and to redeem the lost—those who choose to follow Him. The Bible says: "For the Son of man is come to seek and to save that which was lost" (Luke 19:10). That is Jesus Christ's greatest mission: to find the lost and to redeem them. Jesus Christ is the greatest missionary. He came down to earth from Heaven to endure agony and to suffer death for a guilty human race that He might save them from their sinful and lost condition. "The primary purpose of Christ's coming into the world was to win the lost to personal faith in Himself as the Son of God and savior of man," states Dr. Lehman Trauss (1951:44).

God is offering us a priceless gift—His Son Christ Jesus—in order that, if we believe and accept the gift, we will be saved and will experience the joy of His salvation. For example, if I were to offer you a papaya fruit, I would guarantee you that it is sweet and delicious because I have tasted it. If you won't believe me and will not accept the fruit, you will never experience its taste or enjoy its delicious flavor. Likewise, we will never experience the joy of salvation if we will not believe and accept the gift God is offering to us. The

Bible says: "He that believeth on Him is not condemned: but he that believeth not is condemned already, because he hath not believed in the name of the only begotten Son of God" (John 3:18).

The Wycliffe Bible Commentary states:

The believer in Christ does not come into judgement for his sins either now or in the future... On the other hand, the one who refuses to believe stands judged by virtue of that refusal. He has decided his own fate. That essential idea in judgement is a distinction, a separation...and the coming of Christ as the light proved a great dividing influence. Instead of responding to the love of God by loving His Son, most men loved the darkness in preference to the light because they were attached to their pattern of life which was evil.... (1962:1079).

Children and Ambassadors for Christ

When we say we believe in Jesus Christ as our personal Lord and Savior, it includes receiving Him and becoming the children of God. Not only will we be saved when we believe, but we also will become children of God and ambassadors for Jesus Christ. The Bible says: "For it is by believing in his heart that a man becomes right with God; and with his mouth he tells others of his faith, confirming his salvation" (Rom. 10:10 TLB). In John 1:12 it says: "But as many as received Him, to them gave He power to become the sons of God, even to them that believe on His name."

As trained soul winners, teachers and pastors, we are ambassadors for Christ. As ambassadors, we must be concerned about the plight of the lost souls who do not realize what danger they are in. They need someone to lead and guide them to Jesus Christ as their personal Lord and Savior. That's where we come in as soul winners, teachers and pastors—as ambassadors. The Bible says: "We are Christ's ambassadors. God is using us to speak to you: we beg you, as through Christ Himself were here pleading with you, receive the love He offers you—be reconciled to God. For God took the sinless Christ and poured into Him our sins. Then, in exchange, He poured God's goodness into us" (2 Cor. 5:20,21 TLB). As soul winners, teachers and pastors, our motive is not to exalt ourselves, but to glorify the Lord who alone is to be glorified in all our activities. So we do these things because of what He did for us by saving us.

The Great Commission

As ambassadors, Jesus Christ commissioned us to win, lead and guide the lost souls to faith in Him as their personal Lord and Savior; to teach them to obey all the things Jesus Christ commanded us to do. Jesus says: "Therefore go and make disciples in all the nations, baptizing them into the name of the Father and of the Son and of the Holy Spirit, and then teach these new disciples to obey all the commands I have given you; and be sure of this—that I am with you always, even to the end of the world" (Matt. 28:19,20 TLB).

In this great commission, there are four things that we are to observe as ambassadors. First is "go." We are commanded to go where the lost souls are, to search for them and find them. Jesus Christ set the pattern for us. He came down from Heaven to find and to redeem the lost souls. As soul winners, we are commanded to go, and we must obey His command.

Second is "make disciples." Actually, that means to win the lost souls to faith in Jesus Christ and to a new life in Him. We must go out and tell them how to be saved. When a person believes in his heart, receives Jesus Christ as his personal Lord and Savior, calls upon the Lord in true repentance and confesses his faith in Him, he becomes Christ's disciple.

Third is "baptize." These new converts are to publicly confess Christ Jesus through baptism to show to others that they are saved. It is an act of obedience that follows salvation.

Fourth is "teach." After people have been saved and baptized, we must teach them to obey all the things Jesus Christ commanded us to do. We must also train these people to make disciples who, in turn, teach their converts to go out and make disciples and so forth.

Reproduction

Fruit trees are expected to reproduce and bear fruit. So too are true born again Christians. Once regenerated, we are expected to reproduce. If we do not reproduce, the gospel will die in our generation. As true believers, we are considered Jesus Christ's branches and, as branches, we must bear fruit. Jesus says:

I am the true Vine, and My Father is the Gardener.

He lops off every branch that doesn't produce. And He prunes those branches that bear fruit for even larger crops.

He has already tended you by pruning you back for greater strength and usefulness by means of the commands I gave you.

Take care to live in Me, and let Me live in you. For a branch can't produce fruit when severed from the vine. Nor can you be fruitful apart from Me.

Yes, I am the Vine; you are the branches. Whoever lives in Me and I in him shall produce a large crop of fruit. For apart from Me you can't do a thing.

If anyone separates from Me, he is thrown away like a useless branch, withers, and is gathered into a pile with all the others and bound. (John 15:1-6 TLB)

Therefore, every branch of the true Vine must bear fruit; otherwise, the Lord God will cut it off to be burned. God, the Gardener, will prune the fruit-bearing branch so it will bear more fruit. In like manner, God will prune, rebuke and discpline the fruit-bearing Christians in order to bring more fruit: converts faithful in Jesus Christ.

It is a great honor to be used by the Lord to assist and to promote the growth of the Kingdom of God. It is also a privilege, as a true born again Christian, to serve the Lord in every possible way, through the guidance and direction of the Holy Spirit, for without Him we cannot do anything. We must abide with Him so He will abide with us. We must be filled with the Holy Spirit and be controlled by Him in order to be qualified to assist Him in bringing the unsaved souls to faith in Jesus Christ.

Speaking from experience, personal work produces greater results than other methods of witnessing or soul winning do. Soul winning, however, is to be encouraged no matter what methods are used because it is the only way by which every true believer can participate in reproduction.

Chapter IV

The Soul Winner's Task

Every truly born again Christian is a servant of the Lord God, just as every sinner is a servant of satan. Although any true believer, as a servant, can bear fruit by witnessing for Jesus Christ—like the man possessed by the demon in Mark 5:19—not every believer can win souls for Him. Only those who were trained, whose gifts were developed, and who were chosen, commissioned and ordained by Jesus Christ to do the task of soul winning can be successful in it (John 15:16).

Jesus Christ commanded His converts to follow Him and He would "make [them] to become fishers of men" (Mark 1:17). If they were trained, then they have the knowledge. When they have the knowledge, they are ready to impart that knowledge to anyone who needs salvation. The Bible says: "Quietly trust yourself to Christ your Lord and if anybody asks why you believe as you do, be ready to tell him, and do it in a gentle and respectful way" (1 Pet. 3:15 TLB).

Jesus Set the Pattern

Jesus Christ set the pattern of soul winning for us. The following are a few examples of how Jesus Christ dealt with His first prospects and won them to Himself unto salvation.

1. Jesus called Andrew. Andrew was convicted, then converted, and he believed in Jesus Christ as his personal Lord and Savior. Andrew witnessed to his brother Simon Peter and invited him to Jesus Christ. Simon Peter also was converted, and he believed and followed Him (John 1:40-42).

2. Jesus found Philip. Philip also was converted; he too believed and followed Jesus Christ as his personal Lord and Savior. He then witnessed to Nathanael and invited him to Jesus Christ. So Nathanael also was converted, and he believed and followed Jesus Christ (John 1:43-49).

3. The Samaritan woman went to draw water from the well. Jesus started to converse with her by asking her for a drink, which led them to talk about the living water found in Him, that whoever drinks of that water would never thirst again. The Samaritan woman was converted and, as a result, the whole village was converted by Jesus through the Samaritan woman, who

witnessed to them first and invited them to meet Jesus Christ (John 4:1-30,39).

These are biblical illustrations of the efforts of Jesus Christ Himself in winning lost souls.

Where to Start Soul Winning

As soul winners, we must start in our homes. We must see that every member in our household is converted and enjoying the blessings of Jesus' salvation. One unconverted member of the household may weaken, spoil or even ruin the family Christian fellowship, the family worship or the family reputation. I am inclined to believe that most of the Jewish religious leaders did not believe in Jesus Christ because not one of His brothers or sisters believed in Him. However, they were converted after His resurrection (Acts 1:14).

The Bible in Second Timothy, chapters one and three, give a very good example for parents who lead their children to faith in Jesus Christ as their Lord and Savior. If we follow these examples, patterned by Jesus Christ Himself and by His disciples, then we can do the same thing through the guidance of the Holy Spirit. It is our task as truly born again Christians to witness and to win the lost souls, leading them to a new faith in Jesus Christ and teaching them to bring others to a new faith in Jesus Christ for the glory of His name and for the honor of His Church. An old saying goes: "We are saved to serve." It is wonderful for us to go to Heaven, but it is more wonderful to bring others along with us.

Who Are Chosen and Ordained?

Every true believer who is given the gift of soul winning is chosen and ordained to do the task of soul winning. In other words, every truly born again Christian who has the gift is also selected and appointed by Jesus Christ to do the task of winning souls for Him. Jesus Christ says: "Ye have not chosen Me, but I have chosen you, and ordained you, that ye should go and bring forth fruit, and that your fruit should remain: that whatsoever ye shall ask of the Father in My name, He may give it you" (John 15:16).

Witnessing is the task of the whole Church, the universal Church, the congregation of the born again Christians, and the local church; soul winning is for the chosen and trained believers to do. It is an honor to be chosen to serve Him. However, we should not pride ourselves on being selected and appointed to serve the Lord. Instead, we should humble ourselves and be faithfully obedient to His command. So there are four things to remember and observe in John 15:16. They are:

1. "I have chosen you, and ordained you." It is a great privilege to be selected and appointed to serve the Lord and to participate in the growth of the Kingdom of God. However, if you are chosen or selected to a better or higher position, don't forget those who were left behind.

There was a story about a pauper whose only source of income was the alms from begging. Then he was

The Soul Winner's Task

selected from among dozens of beggars in the city to do errands for a charity organization. All his needs were provided for by this organization, as well as some pocket money. But while living with all the luxuries afforded him, he forgot his colleagues. One day, while walking along the same avenue where he had usually begged for alms, one of his former colleagues approached him. Would the one-time beggar intercede on his former colleague's behalf, that he too might be employed by the same company? But because of pride and of a fear that he might lose his job to the other, the first beggar turned his colleague away. So if you find joy in the Lord, don't be like the pauper. Share it with others and bring them to the Lord with you, so they too can experience the joy of His salvation.

2. "Go and bring forth fruit." That means we must go out with love, proclaiming and leading others to faith in Christ Jesus.

There once was a story about a man who was an animal lover. While out walking one day, he found a skinny, sickly, hungry little dog limping by the roadside. He took the little dog home, nursed it and cared for it. In a week's time, the little dog recovered from its wounds and malnutrition. Now the dog was happy and healthy, playing with his new-found master. But, one day, the little dog disappeared. The master who had nursed and cared for it was disappointed and grumbled to himself: "What an ungrateful animal! After all the things I did for him, he ran away without even saying good-bye." However, one morning he was astonished when he opened the door and found the little dog had returned with four more sickly, hungry dogs.

As truly born again Christians, we too must do the same. We must go out with love and share the message and blessings of salvation to the unsaved souls so they too may experience the joy of His salvation.

3. "That your fruit should remain." As we go out soul winning, we should teach our converts to remain in the faith, to abide in Jesus Christ. He says: "...He that abideth in Me, and I in him, the same bringeth forth much fruit: for without Me ye can do nothing" (John 15:5).

4. "Whatsoever ye shall ask of the Father in My name He may give it you." We love God because He first loved us. To show that we love God, we must abide in His love and our love must abide in Him. In so doing, whatever we ask of Him in the name of His Son, He will give it to us. So as we go out soul winning, we pray because it is the primary thing to do. Also, we do it in faith, believing in the promises of God. We ask the Lord to give us power to defeat satan, the enemy. We must pray that He give to us the right motive in soul winning, which is to worship and glorify Him. We pray to the Lord that He will open the way. We ask the Lord to open the hearts of the prospective converts, and that they would respond to His love and have faith in Jesus Christ. As we pray, we claim His promises and expect wonders. He promised that whatever we ask Him in the

name of His Son, He would give it to us. Let us remember, then, that when we see the miracles that God performs through us in saving souls, we must give Him all the credit and all the glory and honor, for without Him we can do nothing. The conversion of a soul in the family of God is the work of the Holy Spirit through us—the soul winners—whom He controls.

This is our task: to be obedient to the will of God; to be used as an effective instrument in God's hand; to win lost souls for God, who is at work for the glory of His Kingdom.

In closing, I would like to quote from Dr. M.R. Dehaan's book, *Bread for Each Day*. He states:

> There are two ways one can sin with the tongue. The first is well known and recognized by all. It is by "speaking." The use of the tongue for gossip, slander, idle talk, cursing, smutty and suggestive talk is sin. No one will deny this. Our daily prayer should be with David in Psalm 39:1: "I will take heed to my ways, that I sin not with my tongue."
>
> There is, however, another sin of the tongue which is ignored by too many of God's people. It is keeping silent when we ought to speak. It is not usually considered a sin, yet Ezekiel the prophet warns against this in no uncertain words (Ezekiel 3:18,19). If your neighbor's house were afire and you failed to sound an alarm, it would be an inexcusable act. Then why keep silent when those about you are facing eternal fire? (1981:Sept. 7)

Certainly, we are accountable for all our actions. We are our "brothers' keepers." But, if they refuse, we are no longer accountable for their decision.

Chapter V

Qualifications of the Soul Winner

He Must Be a Truly Born Again Christian

Jesus said: "Ye must be born again" (John 3:7b). A soul winner must be a truly born again Christian. He was born physically, but he needs the second birth also, the spiritual birth.

Once again Jesus said: "Verily, verily, I say unto thee, Except a man be born of water and of the Spirit, he cannot enter into the kingdom of God" (John 3:5).

To be born of water (meaning of the flesh) is not enough. A person must be born of the Spirit, or be transformed to a spiritual life. To be "born of the Spirit" is to be "born anew" (John 3:3 RSV) or "born again" (1 Pet. 1:23). That takes place by faith in Jesus Christ through the Holy Spirit. It is by the ministry of the Holy Spirit that we are born again.

The only way we can share a new life with others and win souls for Jesus is to be born anew. We must be transformed by the Holy Spirit in order to enter the Kingdom of God and bring others along with us. We must be born spiritually to be able to have fellowship with God.

Nicodemus was one of the many people who was impressed by the wonders and miracles performed by Jesus Christ. He came to Jesus by night, seeking more information about the way of salvation. We know that Nicodemus was a Pharisee, a ruler of the Jews, a leading teacher of the Jewish people, and a member of the Sanhedrin, the highest council of the Jewish nation.

Why did Nicodemus come to Jesus by night? Maybe considering his position, he didn't want to be seen in public with Jesus Christ. His colleagues might ridicule him and he was not ready to publicly undergo such mockery. Perhaps he came to Jesus by night because Jesus was too busy during the day for an extended inquiry. Whatever the reason, Nicodemus wanted to ask Jesus Christ for more information about the Kingdom of God and his relation to it. But Jesus Christ knew that what Nicodemus needed most was transformation and not information.

If you are not transformed, you cannot understand the message of God. Even a religious leader like Nicodemus was unable to grasp its meaning.

Qualifications of the Soul Winner

Jesus Christ said: "Verily, verily, I say unto thee, Except a man be born of water and of the Spirit, he cannot enter into the kingdom of God" (John 3:5). There are three things to consider in this verse: to be born of water, to be born of the Spirit, and to enter the Kingdom of God.

1. "Born of water." What did Jesus Christ mean by "born of water"? Born of water means physical birth, that which is the normal process in every human birth—being born from the mother's womb. In verse six, Jesus Christ says: "That which is born of the flesh is flesh; and that which is born of the Spirit is spirit." The flesh can reproduce only flesh; likewise the Spirit produces spirit.

Some believe that "born of water" refers to water baptism or Christian baptism. Other denominations believe and teach that new life is obtained by water baptism. Some believe and teach that baptism is related to salvation, based on John 3:5. Another verse they use to establish their allegation is Mark 16:16, which says: "He that believeth and is baptized shall be saved; but he that believeth not shall be damned." But notice the last part of the verse; it says that only those who don't believe shall be condemned. The unbaptized are not included.

The Philippian jailer asked: "Sirs, what must I do to be saved? And they said, Believe on the Lord Jesus Christ, and thou shalt be saved, and thy house" (Acts 16:30,31). The dying thief who hung on a cross at Calvary with Jesus Christ, was saved without water baptism (Luke 23:39-43). Ephesians 2:8 and 9 says: "For by grace are ye saved through faith; and that not of yourselves: it is the gift of God: not of works, lest any man should boast."

Baptism has nothing to do with salvation. The baptism of believers shows to others that they are saved.

2. "Born of the Spirit." This is the second birth: "born anew" or "born from above" or "born again." It comes only through the sacrifice of Jesus Christ on the cross. His blood was shed so you and I could live. Regeneration or new birth is the imputation of divine life into believers.

Mr. James Hastings, editor of "The Great Texts of the Bible," (Vol. 11), writes:

> The new birth is the commencement of a new life. When the child is born it begins to live. No one can tell what mysterious power is that we call life. It is something which all the science of the world is unable either to create or define. Now as life commences in the child at the moment of its birth, so life commences in the soul when it is born again of the Spirit. When new birth is not merely a change of habit in a living soul, it is the commencement of life where there was none before (nd:170).

The new birth introduces divine life into a person's soul. It is the coming of the Holy Spirit within his soul. Without that indwelling of the Holy Spirit, a person cannot be a born again Christian. The Bible says in Romans 8:9: "But ye are not in the flesh, but in the Spirit, if so be that the Spirit of God dwell in you. Now

Qualifications of the Soul Winner

if any man have not the Spirit of Christ, he is none of His."

"New creature" means that the old person has been changed to a new person in Jesus Christ. That is the second birth, becoming born again, or a new creature, as is stated in Second Corinthians 5:17, which says: "Therefore if any man be in Christ, he is a new creature: old things are passed away; behold, all things are become new." That means he has become a new person in Jesus Christ through regeneration or new birth. Again the Bible says: "For we are His workmanship, created in Christ Jesus unto good works, which God hath before ordained that we shall walk in them" (Eph. 2:10).

3. "Enter into the kingdom of God" (salvation by faith). The Bible says: "Except a man be born of water and of the Spirit, he cannot enter into the kingdom of God" (John 3:5). In other words, if a person believes and accept Jesus Christ as his Lord and Savior, he becomes a "new creature," "born again" or "born of the Spirit," meaning he is saved and will enter the Kingdom of God. Unless a person is born again or born or the Spirit, he cannot enter the Kingdom of God. He will never experience the glories of Heaven, or the fellowship with God and the joy of salvation. He cannot witness and lead a lost soul to Jesus Christ. He will never be qualified to be a soul winner.

The new birth, or being born of the Spirit, carries with it eternal life, which is the quality of life that God gives to every true believer. It is not physical, but spiritual life. It is not temporal, but eternal life. It is not human life, but the life that brings about a transformation in the lives of the believers.

A man cannot lead a blind person if he himself is also blind; they will both end up in a ditch. So it is with a sinner. He cannot witness and lead another lost person to Jesus Christ because he himself doesn't know the way. The soul winner must be a born again Christian. As born again Christians, we must win souls to Jesus Christ and help them build up their faith. In the Gospel of Luke, Jesus says to Peter: "But I have prayed for thee, that thy faith fail not: and when thou art converted, strengthen thy brethren" (Luke 22:32).

You must be a born again Christian before you can witness to and win souls and lead them to Jesus Christ. Jesus said: "Ye must be born again" (John 3:7). New birth is necessary to be saved and to enter the Kingdom of God because of the way we came into the world. Without a new birth, we cannot comprehend God's message.

Jesus Christ is the only one who can save you; your religion cannot save you. Even a religious man like Nicodemus could not save himself, unless he became born again. Everyone, including all the members of the Evangelical Church, must be born again to be able to enter the Kingdom of God. There is no other way; there is no detour; Jesus Christ is the only way. Jesus Christ said: "I am the way, the truth, and the life: no man cometh unto the Father, but by Me" (John 14:6). Eternal life is not the state in which we enter into after death, but after regeneration. The Bible says: "He that believeth on the Son hath everlasting life: and he that believeth not the Son shall not see life; but the wrath of God abideth on him" (John 3:36). Once a person is born again, he participates in the life of God. Both the new convert and the saint old in his faith possess eternal life, and both are qualified to witness and to be trained soul winners.

He Must Have Spiritual Communion With God

A soul winner must have a daily communion with God, seeking His guidance and direction through Bible study, devotions and prayer. God promised to answer our prayers and to show us the wonderful things that we don't know. He said: "Call unto Me, and I will answer thee, and shew thee great and mighty things, which thou knowest not" (Jer. 33:3). Jesus Christ said: "If ye abide in Me, and My words abide in you, ye shall ask what ye will, and it shall be done unto you" (John 15:7). Jesus Christ promised every believer that whatever they ask in prayer shall be given to them. He said: "And all things, whatsoever ye shall ask in prayer, believing, ye shall receive" (Matt. 21:22). Also in John 14:13 Jesus Christ said: "And whatsoever ye shall ask in My name, that will I do, that the Father may be glorified in the Son."

These are some of the promises the Lord made to all the true believers or born again Christians, those who call upon Him and commune with Him in prayer, Bible study and devotions. But why is it that we sometimes receive negative answers to our prayers? Is it because God failed in His promises and they are empty and meaningless? Or is it because we are not right with God, and the fault lies in us? We must remember that we are not to dictate what God will do for us. So we pray in Jesus' name and in accordance to God's will: not our will be done, but God's will be done.

In the book "The Perfect Will of God" by the Reverend G. Christian Weiss, the author writes:

> The great heart of God yearns to have His holy will made known and carried out in our lives, and the Spirit of God yearns and groans within our redeemed hearts for the same thing. O, for grace to let Him have full control! When that is the case you may rest assured that God's will shall become a settled matter—doubt, confusion, uncertainty will be swept away (1950:32).

We must remember that all these promises are made with conditions. Yes, there are conditions to be met in order to receive positive answers to our prayers. We must pray in His name and we must pray according to His will.

1. We must pray in His name. We must understand that in every promise, there are conditions. When we pray, we should pray in accordance with these conditions. Then we will receive positive answers.

Let's analyze the words of Jesus when He said: "Verily, verily, I say unto you, He that believeth on Me, the works that I do shall he do also; and greater works than these shall he do; because I go unto My Father" (John 14:12). We, as true believers, must continue the work that was started by Jesus Christ; winning souls to Him, and even working miracles. Jesus is speaking about the extent of work on His behalf, not the quality of work, that is greater. Because He is going to the Father, greater work will be done by the true believer. This work is to be done with Jesus Christ because we cannot do anything apart from Him. Jesus Christ said: "And whatsoever ye shall ask in My name, that I will do, that the Father may be glorified in the Son. If ye shall ask any thing in My name, I will do it" (John 14:13,14).

Praying in His name involves two things: praying in the authority that Jesus Christ gives and praying in union with Him. That way one does not pray outside of His will. If we pray with the authority that Jesus gives and in union with Him, the Father will be glorified in the Son. This, then, is the result of our prayers: to glorify God, to honor Him and to worship Him.

In all our prayers to the Lord, we always conclude with the phrase, "In Jesus' name we pray" or "In Jesus' most precious name we pray." We pray to God through the authority granted to us by Jesus Christ Himself. We pray in union with Jesus, that we will act according to God's will.

2. We must pray according to His will. The Bible says: "And this is the confidence that we have in Him, that, if we ask any thing according to His will, He heareth us: and if we know that He hear us, whatsoever we ask, we know that we have the petitions that we desired of Him" (I John 5:14,15).

John is telling us that God's will is always best for His children. If we pray according to God's will, His promise is to hear us. That also includes the idea that He grants the petitions of our hearts. A truly born again Christian who is in communion with God will not ask anything that is contrary to the will of God.

But how do we know if we are praying according to God's will? Again, we must determine the will of God by communing with Him through prayer, Bible study and devotions. We should take time to pray, to seek God's will, based upon His words. Then, with trust and confidence in Him, we can determine His will.

Now, as soul winners, you and your partner must search the Scriptures together, pray together, and ask the Lord to give you wisdom, knowledge and understanding so you can ascertain His will. We can pray as King David, the psalmist, did: "Open Thou mine eyes, that I may behold wondrous things out of Thy law" (Ps. 119:18). As we go out soul winning, the Lord will guide us and direct us all the way, and show us the wonders of His love. Let us be assured that "the eyes of the Lord are upon the righteous, and His ears are open unto their cry" (Ps. 34:15).

We must remember that we cannot rely on our own strength. In soul winning, we cannot bear fruit without the Lord. He said: "He that abideth in Me, and I in him, the same bringeth forth much fruit: for without Me ye can do nothing" (John 15:5). So we must abide with Him and commune with Him in prayer.

We must pray that the Lord will lead us to the right person. I believe that the Lord wants us to speak to every person with whom we come in contact about the salvation of their souls. I also believe, however, that the Holy Spirit will call us when the harvest in a person is ready. He did so with Philip, when he was called upon to help in the conversion of the Ethiopian eunuch, as well as with Peter, when he was sent to lead Cornelius and his household and friends to Jesus Christ.

We must pray also that the Lord will give us knowledge and wisdom and allow us to use the proper words to communicate the way of salvation and to lead a person to a new life in Jesus Christ. We must pray that the Lord will allow others in the Church to continue the work we started in the hearts of the people in whom we planted the seed of salvation, so they may grow to maturity.

We must remember also that Saint Paul was always remembering and praying for his converts. For example, look at his letter to the Ephesians, when he said: *"cease not to give thanks for you, making mention of you in my prayers, that the God of our Lord Jesus Christ, the Father of glory, may give unto you the spirit of wisdom and revelation in the knowledge of Him"* (Eph. 1:16,17).

The Scriptures teach us that the Holy Spirit will help us when we cannot express ourselves in our prayers. The Bible says: "Likewise the Spirit also helpeth our infirmities: for we know not what we should pray for as we ought: but the Spirit itself maketh intercession for us with groanings which cannot be uttered" (Rom. 8:26). The Lord knows the thoughts and the intentions of our hearts. Even when we compose and express our thoughts as we ought in our prayers, the Holy Spirit will intercede in our behalf.

We will prevail in winning souls, in leading them to Jesus Christ, when we pray in His name and according to His will.

He Must Have Experienced the Spirit-filled Life

Since we are commanded to be filled with the Holy Spirit, then as born again Christians, we must be filled with the Holy Spirit in obedience to His command. We must be "sealed with that holy Spirit of promise" (Eph. 1:13). That means we are sealed by the Holy Spirit into the Body of Christ. Every born again Christian is sealed by the Holy Spirit as being owned by Jesus Christ. We must know also that not every believer is a spiritual Christian. Some are still in the carnal stage of Christian life. They are still babies in the family of God, and are vulnerable to the temptation of sin. However, they are on their way to being filled with the Holy Spirit if they yield to Him and grow into maturity. The Bible says: "And I, brethren, could not speak unto you as unto spiritual, but as unto carnal, even as unto babes in Christ. I have fed you with milk, and not with meat: for hitherto ye were not able to bear it, neither yet now are ye able. For ye are yet carnal: for whereas there is among you envying, and strife, and divisions, are ye not carnal, and walk as men?" (I Cor. 3:1-3)

The Bible teaches us about the character, the condition and the consequence of a Spirit-filled life.

1. The character of a Spirit-filled life. The apostle Paul speaks of being not drunk with wine, but being filled with the Holy Spirit (Eph. 5:18). When one is drunk with wine, he is under the control of the alcohol. Likewise, if a man is filled with the Holy Spirit, he is controlled by the Holy Spirit.

Qualifications of the Soul Winner

When a person believes and accepts Jesus Christ as his personal Lord and Savior, the Holy Spirit automatically dwells in him, but does not control him. We must remember that the Holy Spirit dwells in every believer, but not every believer is controlled by Him. Nevertheless, a believer is expected to be controlled by the Holy Spirit. To be filled with the Holy Spirit is a continuous action in the Christian's life. When sin enters the life of a Christian, the control of the Spirit is broken. Only when the sin is confessed can the Christian be filled again, or controlled again, by the Holy Spirit.

The Wycliffe Bible Commentary states:

No believer in Christ is ever commanded to be indwelt by the Spirit. His indwelling is certain and permanent (Jn. 14:16,17). Nor is a believer commanded to be baptized with the Spirit. This has already been done (1 Cor. 12:13). But believers are commanded to be filled with the Spirit. Hence there is individual responsibility; there are conditions to be met if we are to experience the Spirit's control in our lives (1962:1313).

2. The condition of being filled is obedience to His command. An illustration of this truth is found in Acts 8:29 and 30. This is how the Holy Spirit instructed Philip: "Then the Spirit said unto Philip, Go near, and join thyself to this chariot. And Philip ran thither to him...."

The Holy Spirit does many things. First, He directs God's children. Every believer who desires to be filled or controlled by the Holy Spirit needs direction. That believer must also be willing to be directed. The Holy Spirit uses various ways to give directions.

The Holy Spirit also chooses and commissions workers to serve Him. For an illustration, look at Acts 13:2. The Holy Spirit chose, called and commissioned Barnabas to do the work He had been preparing for him to do.

The Holy Spirit teaches the truth about Christ Jesus. In John 14:26, Jesus Christ said: "But the Comforter, which is the Holy Ghost, whom the Father will send in My name, He shall teach you all things, and bring all things to your remembrance, whatsoever I have said unto you."

The Holy Spirit also reproves sinners, and convicts them of their sins. Jesus said: "And when He is come, He will reprove the world of sin..." (John 16:8). Sin is the refusal to accept Jesus Christ and His message. But the Lord recognizes sin in His children's lives and made provision for it. In return, He expects His children to respond to His love and grace.

3. The consequence of being Spirit-filled is the evidence of fruit. As a result of Philip's obedience, the Ethiopian eunuch was led to Jesus Christ, accepting Him as his personal Lord and Savior. The eunuch said: "I believe that Jesus Christ is the Son of God" (Acts 8:37). So he then was baptized and became the second gentile convert according to Luke. Nicolas of Antioch was the first convert (Acts 6:5).

Fruit becomes visible as a result of being Spirit-filled. The Bible says: "But when the Holy Spirit controls our lives He will produce this kind of fruit in us:

love, joy, peace, patience, kindness, goodness, faithfulness, gentleness and self-control; and here there is no conflict with Jewish laws" (Gal. 5:22,23 TLB).

Worship and praise are produced as a result of being Spirit-filled. Worship is the outward expression of praise and the inner expression of melody-making in the heart. It makes a grateful and thankful heart, when it is controlled and directed by the Holy Spirit. Dr. Billy Graham writes:

> ...we must remember that the filling of the Spirit does not mean we are perfect and without sin. It means we are controlled by the Spirit, but sin is still a reality, lurking around the corner ready to lunge at the first opportunity. We may be blameless in our desire to serve Christ, but that does not make us without fault (1978:177,178).

One of the greatest needs of the world today is for every one of God's children to experience the Spirit-filled life. That is, to be controlled and directed by the Holy Spirit, to win lost souls to a new life in Jesus Christ and to experience the joy of His salvation.

He Must Have a Burden for Souls

A soul winner must have a heavy burden in his heart for lost souls. Jesus had, especially for His own people in the city of Jerusalem. The Gospel of Luke says: "And when He was come near, He beheld the city, and wept over it" (Luke 19:41). Jesus Christ said: "O Jerusalem, Jerusalem, thou that killest the prophets, and stonest them which are sent unto thee, how often would I have gathered thy children together, even as a hen gathereth her chickens under her wings, and ye would not!" (Matt. 23:37)

The apostle Paul also displayed deep love and concern for lost souls when he said: "That I have great heaviness and continual sorrow in my heart. For I could wish that myself were accursed from Christ for my brethren, my kinsmen according to the flesh" (Rom. 9:2,3).

While witnessing to a crowd one day, a minister told about the heavy burden in his heart for the lost souls. A man in the crowd stood up and said, "I have been going to church like you, but I don't feel any burden in my heart."

The minister asked him politely, "If I put a heavy load over a dead body, will the dead person feel the heavy load on himself?"

"Definitely not," answered the man. "He is dead."

"In like manner," the minister said, "when you are dead spiritually, you don't feel any burden at all because you are dead in your sins. For the Bible says: 'For the wages of sin is death' (Rom. 6:23). If you are a sinner, you are dead spiritually."

The man protested and said, "But I am not a sinner!"

The minister quoted Romans 3:23 and said, "But the Bible says: 'For all have sinned, and come short of the glory of God.' In verse 10 it says: 'There is none righteous, no not one.' I am a sinner, you are a sinner, everybody is a sinner." The minister continued and referred the man to Romans 6:23 and said: "But the gift of God is eternal life through Jesus Christ our Lord." He admonished the crowd and said: "If you have eternal life, share it with others so they too might experience the joy of salvation."

As born again Christians, we are to be concerned about the plight of lost souls. We witness to them, win them and lead them to Jesus Christ to be their personal Lord and Savior. No matter how insignificant we feel ourselves to be or how limited we feel our talents are, that will not prevent us from the privilege of witnessing for Jesus Christ, like the man once possessed by a demon (Mark 5:1-20). No matter how small our gifts are, we can still be trained to win the lost souls and lead them to Jesus Christ as their personal Lord and Savior, like Philip, who led the Ethiopian eunuch to Jesus Christ (Acts 8:26-38).

If we really feel a heavy burden for lost souls, we must find them, guide them and lead them to Jesus Christ. We should ask everyone whom we come in contact with where they are bound. If they were to die now, where will they go? I know it is embarrassing to ask such questions, but we won't know if they need salvation or not unless we ask. It is not easy to ask them these questions. They might say we are crazy, and nobody likes to be called crazy. But that's the only way by which we can discern their needs. If we really care, we must do it for their sake.

A minister shared with me his experiences in the ministry of the Lord. At one time he was a pastor of a small church in a small village. Almost all the residents in that village were members of his church, but only a few attended the church services. Most of the people entered the church only three times during their lives: first when they were baptized; second when they were married; and third when they were dead, in a funeral service.

The people's only source of livelihood was farming. The pastor was a self-supporting minister, so had to farm too, to support his family. After the harvest, the farmers had to dry their crops in the fields for a month's time or more before they could store it in their granaries. The farmers had to guard their produce because the crops grew legs and walked away and disappeared during the night. So the pastor had to watch his crops too.

One moonlit night, while the pastor was meditating, communing with God in prayer inside his shelter of hay, he felt a heavy burden in his heart for the souls of his people. He prayed and asked God what he could do to bring his people to truly believe in Jesus Christ as their personal Lord and Savior.

All of a sudden, he thought of his sermon for the next Lord's day. He decided to practice the delivery of it. So he went outside his hut and started practicing his message at the top of his voice. After finishing his introduction, he said, "To you unseen creatures, come out now and reason with me, for you need the salvation of your souls. Come out from your hiding places." Before he even finished the last phrase, he saw a figure appearing from a distance, moving toward him. Then another

Qualifications of the Soul Winner

from another direction, then another and another, all coming closer. But they stopped at a distance. They came just as close as necessary, to where they could understand what he was yelling about. This minister thought he was seeing a company of ghosts. Although he trusted the Lord God, fear crept into his body. He felt his hair stand up; he felt his head grow five times bigger. He felt hot, as with the heat of a furnace, but his body was as cold as ice.

Nevertheless, he continued delivering his prepared message, from which he unknowingly deviated. He quoted the Bible from memory and said, "The Bible in Romans 3:23 says: 'For all have sinned, and come short of the glory of God,' and Romans 3:10 says: 'There is none righteous, no, not one.' All are sinners and no one is righteous. That includes me and you." Then he asked them a question, and said, "What did sin do for us? Sin brought death to us all. For the Bible says in Romans 6:23: 'For the wages of sin is death,' which means death spiritually or death in hell. Although we are sinners, and we are spiritually dead, we will have eternal life if we believe and accept the free gift of God the Father, which is Jesus Christ His only Son. The Bible says: 'But the gift of God is eternal life through Jesus Christ our Lord' (Rom. 6:23). John 3:16 says: 'For God so loved the world, that He gave His only begotten Son, that whosoever believeth in Him should not perish, but have everlasting life.' And Ephesians 2:8 and 9 says: 'For by grace are ye saved through faith; and that not of yourselves: it is the gift of God: not of works, lest any man should boast.' Now if you want to go to hell, stay where you are, but if you want to go to Heaven, come forward and accept Jesus Christ as your Lord and Savior right now, for He will gladly forgive you of your sins, and be saved."

Then this minister quoted another verse and said, "In Romans 5:8 the Bible says: 'But God commendeth His love toward us, in that, while we were yet sinners, Christ died for us.' That means He paid the price or penalty for our sins, because the wages of sin is death. He died for you and me."

So he then quoted Romans 10:9 and said, "The Bible says: 'That if thou shalt confess with thy mouth the Lord Jesus, and shalt believe in thine heart that God hath raised Him from the dead, thou shalt be saved.' According to this verse, there are two things you should do to be saved. First, 'thou shalt confess' means you have to trust the Lord with your heart, and with your mouth you must declare that Jesus Christ is your Lord and Savior. Second, 'thou shalt believe' means you must, in your heart, believe that God raised Jesus from the dead. You must also accept Him as your Lord and Savior. If you do that, 'thou shalt be saved.' I challenge every one of you now to come forward to confess and to believe and experience the joy of His salvation."

While he was extending this invitation, the figures again started to move toward him. To his surprise, as they stood closely enough before him to be recognized, he realized that they were human beings. Almost all of them were from his village. He led them to truly confess, believe and accept Jesus Christ as their Lord and Savior.

The Sunday following that incident was thanksgiving Sunday. The villagers came to church with their families. The people also brought a portion of their crops and presented to the Lord in thanksgiving. It was the first time that the people had flocked to the church since it was established. It was the answer to his prayers.

God really answers prayers in marvelous ways. In Jeremiah 33:3 it says: "Call unto Me, and I will answer thee, and shew thee great and mighty things, which thou knowest not."

Chapter VI

Methods of Soul Winning

There are several practical methods of soul winning that are commonly practiced by members of several churches. These methods have resulted from many years of experience. They go out in twos as demonstrated by Jesus Christ when He sent His disciples in teams of twos. According to the Gospel of Luke: "After these things the Lord appointed other seventy also, and sent them two and two before His face into every city and place, whither He Himself would come" (10:1).

Although an individual out soul winning has good results, there are inevitable drawbacks that hurt his efforts in soul winning. Experience has proven that soul winning teams of two have better results. Teams of two men should deal with men, and teams of two women should deal with women. But, when dealing with a whole family, the husband and wife team is the most effective in soul winning.

Soul Winning in the Home

As soul winners, we must start witnessing from within our own homes. Unconverted members of our family must be led to Jesus Christ first, before we go out winning other souls for Him. The members of our household should be our first priorities, then our relatives and friends, then others. How wonderful it would be if the whole family unitedly prayed and worshiped the Lord of hosts. How wonderful it would be to have a church in the home, where the father is the preacher and the whole household is the congregation.

The Holy Spirit used Peter as an instrument in the conversion of Cornelius and his household. Cornelius and his household were very religious, yet they didn't have the assurance of salvation. The Holy Spirit used Cornelius as a channel in the conversion of his household, his family, relatives and friends, through the guidance of the Holy Spirit. The results were great because those efforts of Peter and Cornelius were made in the strength of the Holy Spirit. (See Acts 10.)

Witnessing to the right prospects in their homes, at the right time, at the time of harvest, produces great results. They will welcome you with open arms. They are only too glad to have you in their homes, if only to pray with them and for them. Witness to them and lead them to Jesus Christ as their personal Lord and Savior. Invite them to church and they will willingly come, to confess Jesus Christ as their personal Lord and Savior. Like Cornelius and his household when they welcomed Peter and his companions, they will readily submit themselves for baptism to show that they are saved.

There are times, though, when you encounter some difficulties. That is when the time is not right and the harvest is not yet ready. You are not welcome in their homes. They are too busy working for their worldly treasures, with no time for God and heavenly treasures. When you are not welcome in their homes, graciously accept it and say: "Thank you, God bless you, good-bye." Then leave immediately.

You could request a brief prayer, and say: "Would you mind if we pray for you before we leave?" If the answer is positive, pray for the salvation of their souls; that they too will experience the joy of His salvation. After the prayer, be polite and say: "Thank you, God bless you, good-bye." Then leave immediately.

Soul Winning at the Sickbed

One of the soft spots of soul winning is at the sickbed in the hospital or in the home. Witnessing to prospects on their sickbeds has great results. That is the time they need to be very close to God, for help and physical healing. But most importantly of all, they need the healing of their sin-sick souls. So lead them to Jesus Christ for the salvation of their souls. Show them the wonderful ministries of Jesus, who performed miracles of healing, by reading one or more of the following scriptures:

And, behold, there came a leper and worshipped Him, saying, Lord, if Thou wilt, Thou canst make me clean.

And Jesus put forth His hand, and touched him, saying, I will; be thou clean. And immediately his leprosy was cleansed. (Matt. 8:2,3)

And when Jesus was come into Peter's house, He saw his wife's mother laid, and sick of a fever.

And He touched her hand, and the fever left her: and she arose, and ministered unto them. (Matt. 8:14,15)

And, behold, a woman, which was diseased with an issue of blood twelve years, came behind Him, and touched the hem of His garment:

For she said within herself, If I may but touch His garment, I shall be whole.

But Jesus turned Him about, and when He saw her, He said, Daughter, be of good comfort; thy faith hath made thee whole. And the woman was made whole from that hour. (Matt. 9:20-22)

Other scriptures include the following:
1. Jesus healed the servant of the captain (Luke 7:1-10).
2. Jesus raised the dead girl (Matt. 9:18-26; Luke 8:40-56).
3. Jesus made the blind see and the dumb talk (Matt. 9:27-34).

Then pray for that person who is ill. Intercede on his behalf and on his family's. Those who become healed will surrender their lives to Jesus Christ. The Lord needs the testimonies of born again Christians who will tell what wonderful things He did for their lives during their hours of agony.

Mr. Ralph W. Rusthoi has some tips to observe when visiting a sick prospect in the hospital. He writes: "If [a] call is to be made in a hospital, get permission of the attendants or those in charge. Keep [the] rules of [the] hospital or institution, do not forget that you are there to bring comfort from the Word of God, do not meddle into their medical care.

Method

1. Arrange for your visit, if possible; go when it is most convenient for [the] sick person.
2. Enter quietly, use [a] soft voice and gentle manner.
3. Have compassion, not pity, [and] make [the] visit short.
4. Do not speak on any subject that you know will upset [the] patient.
5. Help in any other way that you can.
6. Make him feel that he has a real friend in you and can call on you any time of day or night for prayer or help in [an] emergency.
7. Give comfort[ing] Scriptures, also assurance of God's faithfulness. Some are sorely tried even about their soul's salvation during their illness. Satan plants many doubts, [and] he strikes when one is down in body.
8. Read from the Bible and have prayer. Be wise in your prayer" (1960:51).

Soul Winning at the Workplace

Truly born again Christians who own business corporations could open their businesses with five-minute prayer meetings. They could also witness to their employees and lead them to Jesus Christ as their Lord and Savior, as soul winners. Soul winners could also witness to their co-workers, during breaks or during lunch, and hopefully lead them to the Lord and Savior Jesus Christ. But remember, do not use the company's hours to witness and win souls.

Soul Winning Through Radio and TV Ministries

Although radio and television ministry is expensive, a few can afford to use it. We should mention its great success; a great number of souls have been won to Jesus Christ since the TV ministries' very beginnings. Those who may not be reached by the Church through soul winners may be reached and touched through radio and television ministry.

Soul Winning at Anniversary and Birthday Parties

A husband and wife team may invite their prospects as well as their friends on their wedding anniversary or on their birthdays for a thanksgiving service led by their minister. It may be the first time some are exposed to the preaching of the Word of God or to the atmosphere of a worship service. So here, in an anniversary service, they will get their first contact with the Church and its message. Here, you can have opened wide the way and the opportunity to visit them at their homes and win them to Jesus Christ as their Lord and Savior.

Methods of Soul Winning

The local church cannot survive without soul winners. The strength of the local church lies in the efforts of all members witnessing, soul winning and discipling for Christ Jesus. That is the secret of the local church's success.

Caution: Do not attempt to convert those who have already been converted just because their beliefs differ from yours about the observance of the Lord's Supper or the mode of baptism. These sacraments have nothing to do with salvation. You are just wasting time and effort. You will never have a crown or a reward from God even if you proselytized thousands of them.

To determine whether the prospect is saved or not, ask him: "Where will you spend eternity when you leave this world?" You will know by his answer if he has the assurance of salvation or not. If he is a truly born again Christian, then politely say: "God bless you, good-bye," and then leave immediately.

Chapter VII

The Approach

First of all, we must remember that we do all these things not to save ourselves, but because we have already been saved. We do them not to exalt ourselves, but to thank God and to glorify Him for His love and grace that He bestowed on us. We do them in obedience to His command (Matt. 28:19,20).

When I was young in the ministry, I was not fully aware about the aspects of soul winning. I didn't know how to do it. I was trained at seminary to preach and to administer a church, but not to win the lost souls.

However, as part of my ministry, I had to go out and visit the members and non-members; praying for them, witnessing and inviting them to church. As a result, many were converted and joined the church. That gave me incentive and encouragement to do more visiting, witnessing and praying with and for people; then inviting them to church.

Years later, I discovered that it was the Holy Spirit who convicted, converted and led them to Christ Jesus as their personal Lord and Savior. I was used only as an instrument to introduce them to Jesus Christ as their Savior and Lord. This realization encouraged me to search the Scriptures and other materials about soul winning. I studied and applied the different ideas and suggestions of methods of and approach to soul winning from all the materials available, to which I am gratefully indebted. With the knowledge acquired through research, added to my years of practical experience, and with the guidance of the Holy Spirit, I was able to determine what was needed in each situation and I shaped my own ways and methods of approach that produced the greatest results.

How to Deal With the Situation When It Seems Difficult

With trust and confidence in God's guidance and direction, we must go through the obstacles with understanding, common sense and a prayerful spirit.

That is how Jesus Christ dealt with difficulties. Although Jesus was rejected when He came to His hometown, He handled the situation with care. He walked through the crowd and went away. Luke describes it in this way: "But He passing through the midst of them went His way" (Luke 4:30).

The Approach

Since we cannot do anything without Him, we must pray that the Holy Spirit would empower us to do the task and direct us to the right prospect. We pray as we bring the message of salvation to the people, that God would open their hearts. If they respond positively, God will save them. We must remember that nothing is impossible with God. Jesus said: "With men it is impossible, but not with God: for with God all things are possible" (Mark 10:27).

Where to Find the Prospects

Jesus found them everywhere. Everywhere Jesus Christ went, He found someone to save and to forgive. This is how good Luke describes it: "For the Son of man is come to seek and to save that which was lost" (Luke 19:10).

Based on Jesus' example, we find our prospects throughout our daily life. As a soul winner, we are in touch with them in the world in which we live in our daily life in a wonderful way. Perhaps our prospects are right in front of our noses. So wherever we are, we will find lost souls right before our eyes. Remember that every person with whom we come in contact is a prospect, a person who needs the Lord.

List the Prospects

Before you and your partner go out winning souls for Jesus Christ, the two of you should make a list of all the prospects you know. Start with the closest unsaved family members, then relatives, friends and acquaintances. Pray for them and, as you pray, present and dedicate them to the Lord. However, concentrate on one individual or one family at a time.

Pray for Them and for God's Leading

Pray for the prospects daily, as well as for God's leading and guidance. Begin to have a closer contact with them. Associate with them and let them know you are really concerned and care for them. Pursue a closer friendship with them; win their trust and confidence. I know it is a slow approach, but it is sure, almost 100 percent sure. So pray that the Lord will prepare the way and open their hearts. As you pray, always listen and feel the urgings of the Holy Spirit. Be open like Peter, when the Holy Spirit instructed him to lead Cornelius and his household to Jesus Christ (Acts 10). Be like Philip when the Holy Spirit directed him to find the Ethiopian eunuch and then used him to lead the eunuch to Jesus Christ as his personal Lord and Savior (Acts 8:26,39).

We will start to move when we are certain that the time is right, when the field is ready for harvest. However, we know that we cannot do it alone. Without the Holy Spirit preparing both the way and the harvest, our effort will be in vain. It would be a failure apart from Him. So we must rely on the Holy Spirit for strength, guidance and direction. Are you not glad when you have a part in the salvation of a lost soul? Of course every soul winner must be happy. Even the heavenly host rejoices for every soul that is won to Jesus Christ. The Bible says: "Likewise, I say unto you there is joy in the presence of the angels of God over one sinner that repenteth" (Luke 15:10). Mr. Lehman Strauss writes:

> How blessed it is indeed to be so led by the Holy Spirit that we ourselves can lead others without difficulty!...
>
> When the Holy Spirit calls men and sends them forth to do a social work, those men can count upon guidance to the places where they should visit. The Spirit, knowing when and where to send the servant of the Lord, will not allow him to travel the path of his own choosing, provided he is a ready and willing listener to the divine voice (1961:63,66,67).

Soul winners are sent to do a special task; where the Holy Spirit leads, they must follow and listen to the call. With these thoughts in mind, we could çall them missionaries, since they are called and sent on a mission.

The duty for each member of the soul winning team should be prearranged, as to who will lead and do the talking. The other partner will assist the prospect in finding the verses referred to in the Bible.

Only one of the team should do the talking. The partner must not interrupt by joining in the conversation, say for instance, at the opening of the conversation that eventually would lead them to talk about the prospect's salvation. If the partner interferes, most of the time it hinders them from leading the prospect to Jesus Christ. It also is a waste of time.

The partner must not interrupt by arguing with the leader if he disagrees. It is not a Bible study. If he does so, he will drive the prospect away.

I went out soul winning one day with a fellow minister from another group, but he didn't know about soul winning. Instead of assisting the prospect, he was busy marking his Bible. When he disagreed he argued with me, making the prospect confused.

Let the leader do the talking and present God's plan of salvation. The partner must see to it that the meeting is not interrupted. If somebody knocks at the door or a telephone rings, the partner can answer the call politely and say that they are having a very important meeting and that they cannot be disturbed. The partner then assists the prospect all the way through the process.

Chapter VIII

Soul Winning Procedure

Each soul winner has different procedures in winning lost souls. As a result of their knowledge and wisdom, derived from searching the Scriptures and books by great minds and with the years of experience, they have discovered their own procedures that provide them with a greater harvest.

I discovered that the following procedure is the most effective one for me in winning lost souls to Jesus Christ as their personal divine Lord and Savior.

God's Plan of Salvation

A. Believe

Lead the prospect to believe:

1. That the Bible is the Word of God. If the prospect really believes, he will follow God's instruction and discipline for righteousness. The Bible says:

All scripture is given by inspiration of God, and is profitable for doctrine, for reproof, for correction, for instruction in righteousness. (II Tim. 3:16)

But these are written, that ye might believe that Jesus is the Christ, the Son of God; and that believing ye might have life through His name. (John 20:31)

2. That all are sinners and no one is righteous.

As it is written, There is none righteous, no, not one. (Rom. 3:10)

For all have sinned, and come short of the glory of God. (Rom. 3:23)

3. That the wages of sin is death, which is separation from God. It is the spiritual death or the second death.

For the wages of sin is death. (Rom. 6:23a)

And death and hell were cast into the lake of fire. This is the second death. (Rev. 20:14)

But the fearful, and unbelieving, and the abominable, and murderers, and whoremongers, and sorcerers, and idolaters, and all liars, shall have their part in the lake which burneth with fire and brimstone: which is the second death. (Rev. 21:8)

4. That God loves us all and made a way of escape for us, whereby we could avoid the second death. The following verses assure us of these facts.

For God so loved the world, that He gave His only begotten Son, that whosoever believeth in Him should not perish, but have everlasting life. (John 3:16)

But the gift of God is eternal life through Jesus Christ our Lord. (Rom. 6:23b)

5. That Jesus Christ is the only way to the Father. There is no other way. Jesus Christ said:

I am the way, the truth, and the life: no man cometh unto the Father, but by Me. (John 14:6)

6. That while we were still sinners, Jesus Christ died for our sins. Saint Paul included himself as one of those sinners.

But God commendeth His love toward us, in that, while we were yet sinners, Christ died for us. (Rom. 5:8)

7. That all believers are not condemned, while the non-believers are already condemned.

He that believeth on Him is not condemned: but he that believeth not is condemned already, because he hath not believed in the name of the only begotten Son of God. (John 3:18)

8. That salvation is a gift from God through faith. You cannot buy it, neither can you work for it. It is a gift.

For by grace are ye saved through faith; and that not of yourselves: it is the gift of God:

Not of works, lest any man should boast. (Eph. 2:8,9)

Not by works of righteousness which we have done, but according to His mercy He saved us, by the washing of regeneration, and renewing of the Holy Ghost. (Titus 3:5)

9. That salvation cannot be obtained by the observance of the law.

Knowing that a man is not justified by the works of the law, but by the faith of Jesus Christ, even we have believed in Jesus Christ, that we might be justified by the faith of Christ, and not by the works of the law: for by the works of the law shall no flesh be justified. (Gal. 2:16)

10. That Jesus Christ is the only Lord and Savior by which he can be saved. He just needs to believe and trust the only Savior.

...Sirs, what must I do to be saved?

And they said, Believe on the Lord Jesus Christ, and thou shalt be saved, and thy house. (Acts 16:30,31)

B. Receive

When a person believes in Jesus Christ, he must also receive Him. He is the priceless gift of God the Father to all of us. It is interesting to note, that satan also believes, but that he is in terror. The Bible says:

Thou believest that there is one God; thou doest well: the devils also believe, and tremble. (James 2:19)

1. Lead the prospect to receive Jesus Christ in order for him to become a child of God. The Bible says:

But as many as received Him, to them gave He power to become the sons of God, even to them that believe on His name. (John 1:12)

Soul Winning Procedure

2. Lead the prospect to open his heart and to invite Jesus Christ to come into his life. Jesus the Lord and Savior said:

Behold, I stand at the door, and knock: if any man hear My voice, and open the door, I will come in to him, and will sup with him, and he with Me. (Rev. 3:20)

C. Repent

When a person truly believes and receives Jesus Christ as his personal Lord and Savior, he must also repent from his sins and be willing to start a new life with Jesus Christ, for he will not perish.

I tell you, Nay: but except ye repent, ye shall all likewise perish. (Luke 13:3)

Repent ye therefore, and be converted, that your sins may be blotted out, when the times of refreshing shall come from the presence of the Lord. (Acts 3:19)

The Manifestation of Salvation

When a person believes and receives Jesus Christ as his personal Lord and Savior, he becomes saved. Now, as a believer, he must be baptized in obedience to Jesus' command.

And Jesus came and spake unto them, saying, All power is given unto Me in heaven and in earth.

Go ye therefore, and teach all nations, baptizing them in the name of the Father, and of the Son, and of the Holy Ghost:

Teaching them to observe all things whatsoever I have commanded you: and, lo, I am with you alway, even unto the end of the world. Amen. (Matt. 28:18-20)

Therefore, baptism is the act of the believer in obedience to the command of Jesus Christ.

1. Baptism

a. Water baptism. The water baptism of the believers shows that they have been saved. For example, take the following instances:

1) The baptism of the Philippian jailer. After his conversion, he was baptized immediately, along with his family.

Then they spoke the word of the Lord to him and to all the others in his house.

At that hour of the night the jailer took them and washed their wounds; then immediately he and all his family were baptized. (Acts 16:32,33 NIV)

2) The baptism of Cornelius, his family, relatives and friends. After they became converted and received the Holy Ghost, they were baptized by Peter.

Peter asked, "Can anyone object to my baptizing them, now that they have received the Holy Spirit just as we did?"

So he did, baptizing them in the name of Jesus, the Messiah. (Acts 10:47,48 TLB)

3) The baptism of Paul. Just after Paul's conversion, he was baptized by Ananias in the house of Judas, where Paul had been praying to the Lord.

Immediately, something like scales fell from Saul's eyes, and he could see again. He got up and was baptized,

and after taking some food, he regained his strength. (Acts 9:18,19 NIV)

b) Baptism of the Holy Spirit. The baptism of the Holy Spirit takes place as soon as you believe and receive Jesus Christ as your personal Lord and Savior. The following verse indicates that believers from the different walks of life were baptized with the Holy Spirit and that it was never to be repeated upon them.

Each of us is a part of the one body of Christ. Some of us are Jews, some are Gentiles, some are slaves and some are free. But the Holy Spirit has fitted us all together into one body. We have been baptized into Christ's body by the one Spirit, and have all been given that same Holy Spirit. (1 Cor. 12:13 TLB)

Some mistakenly interpret receiving the gift of the Holy Spirit or being filled with and controlled by the Holy Spirit as the baptism of the Holy Spirit. Many believers were baptized with the Holy Spirit, but never filled or controlled by the Holy Spirit. The New Testament Christians were not told to seek the baptism of the Holy Spirit that the believers already had. There is no command in the New Testament by which Christians are commanded to be baptized with the Holy Spirit.

The baptism of the Holy Spirit as a corporate body was given once to the Church. It was given once to:

1) The Jewish believers. The Jews were the chosen people of God. With this thought in mind the Jews

looked down on the Gentiles. Even the followers of Jesus did not eat and fellowship with the Gentiles.

These Jewish believers were not immediately baptized with the Holy Spirit when they were converted to a new life in Jesus Christ. The Holy Spirit had not come down yet at that time. Jesus Christ told His disciples that they would be baptized soon.

> *For John truly baptized with water, but ye shall be baptized with the Holy Ghost not many days hence.* (Acts 1:5)

> *And, behold, I send the promise of My Father upon you: but tarry ye in the city of Jerusalem, until ye be endued with power from on high.* (Luke 24:49)

When Jesus Christ ascended to Heaven to be with the Father, He sent down the Holy Spirit, who came down on the day of Pentecost. That was 50 days after His resurrection, or 10 days after His ascension.

On the day of Pentecost, all the believers were baptized with the Holy Spirit into the body of Jesus Christ.

> *And suddenly there came a sound from heaven as of a rushing mighty wind, and it filled all the house where they were sitting.*

> *And there appeared unto them cloven tongues like as of fire, and it sat upon each of them.*

> *And they were all filled with the Holy Ghost, and began to speak with other tongues, as the Spirit gave them utterance.* (Acts 2:2-4)

They were not only baptized with the Holy Spirit, they also were filled with the Holy Spirit and spoke in tongues, or in languages they did not know. The Jewish people born in other countries who came to celebrate the feast of Pentecost were amazed, for they heard these disciples speak their languages (Acts 2:5-12).

The day of Pentecost was the birth of the Christian Church and Jesus Christ is the head of the Church. The event that took place during the day of Pentecost was a wonder and a miracle; the roaring of the wind revealing the coming of the Holy Spirit, the appearance of the tongue-like fire signifying the preaching of the gospel of Jesus Christ, and the fire symbolizing the power and zeal given to those who believed and obeyed Jesus' command. The *Wycliffe Bible Commentary* states:

> As the Holy Spirit was given to men, the disciples were baptized (1:5) and at the same time filled with the Holy Spirit. The baptism of the Holy Spirit is described in I Cor. 12:13. It is the work of the Holy Spirit to join people of diverse racial and social backgrounds into one body—the body of Jesus Christ, which is his Church. In the strict sense of the word, Pentecost was the birthday of the Church. This baptism of the Spirit was never repeated. It was later extended to believers in Samaria (Acts 8), to the Gentiles (chs. 10; 11), and to the disciples of John the Baptist (19:1-6). The filling of the Spirit was often repeated, but not the baptism with the Spirit (1962:1126,27).

2) The Samaritan Believers. The Samaritans were a people of mixed blood—of the Gentiles and the Jews. The Israelites looked down on them, and despised them as the lowest class of people. Still, when Philip

preached Jesus Christ to them, they readily believed and accepted Jesus Christ as their personal Lord and Savior. Philip then baptized them in the name of Jesus Christ (Acts 8:5-13).

The apostles in Jerusalem learned about the Samaritans who were baptized by Philip, so they sent Peter and John to verify the news. Peter and John found out that it was true and prayed for the Samaritan believers, that they might receive the Holy Spirit. Peter and John laid their hands on the Samaritan converts and they received the Holy Spirit (Acts 8:14-17). The Wycliffe Bible Commentary further states:

> The significance of this event lies in the fact that these people were Samaritans. Here is the first step in which the church burst its Jewish bonds and moved toward a truly world-wide fellowship. The imposition of hands was not necessary for the Samaritans; but it was necessary for the apostles, that they might be fully convinced that God was indeed breaking the barriers of racial prejudice and including these half-breed people within the fellowship of the Church. This was not a new Pentecost but an extension of the one Pentecost to Samaritan people (1962:1139).

This fact shows that even the lowest class of people becomes God's people by faith in Christ Jesus. Without these events, the laying on of hands and the receiving of the Holy Spirit, the Jewish Christians would never have been convinced that God loved the Samaritans too.

3) The Gentile Converts. The Gentiles are another class of people despised by the Jews. As soon as

the Gentiles believed and received Jesus Christ as their personal Lord and Savior, they too received the Holy Spirit and spoke in tongues (Acts 10:44-48).

If the Gentiles had not spoken in tongues and received the Holy Spirit, the Jewish Christians would never have believed that the Gentiles also could become a part of God's people. They would never have believed that the love of God extended to the Gentiles too. The Bible says: "While Peter yet spake these words, the Holy Ghost fell on all them which heard the word" (Acts 10:44).

The *Wycliffe Bible Commentary* provides additional facts about the Gentiles who received the Holy Ghost:

> On the day of Pentecost, Peter had exhorted his hearers to repent, to be baptized for the forgiveness of sins, and to receive the Holy Spirit (2:38). At Caesarea, this order of events was changed, and the Holy Spirit fell upon Cornelius and his family before they were baptized. This was not a new Pentecost but an extension of Pentecost to include the Gentiles (1962:1143).

4) The Disciples of John the Baptist. The 12 disciples of John were found by Paul while he was preaching at Ephesus. Their knowledge about the Holy Spirit and of Jesus Christ was incomplete. They were only baptized by John with the baptism of repentance. So Paul preached Jesus Christ unto them, and when they believed and accepted Jesus as their Lord and Savior, Paul baptized them in the name of Jesus. Then Paul laid his hands on their heads, the Holy Spirit came on them, and they spoke in other languages and prophesied (Acts 19:1-7).

These disciples of John were a distinct group; their baptism with the Holy Spirit was delayed, pending their acceptance of Jesus Christ as Savior. Let us look again at what the *Wycliffe Bible Commentary* says in this matter.

This does not describe a new Pentecost but an extension of the Pentecostal experience to include all believers. No special significance is to be sought in the imposition of Paul's hands for the bestowal of the Spirit. This experience, like that of Peter and John in Samaria (8:16,17), is designed to illustrate the oneness of the Church. Since believers are baptized by one Spirit into one body (1 Cor. 12:13), there can be no such "splinter groups" as these disciples of John outside the Church (1962:1160).

We can clearly see now that the baptism with the Holy Spirit happened only once to the Church, the believers as a whole. During the day of Pentecost, all the believers were Jews, the chosen people (Acts 2:2-4). However, the Pentecost, the baptism with the Holy Spirit, was extended to all believers outside the Jewish nation. It was extended once to the Samaritans (Acts 8:14-17); once to the Gentiles (Acts 10:44-48); and once to the disciples of John the Baptist, who were Jews and who were supposed to be with the believers at the day of Pentecost (Acts 2:2-4). However, their baptism with the Holy Spirit was delayed because their knowledge of Jesus Christ and of the Holy Spirit were incomplete. So, when Paul preached Jesus Christ and laid his hands on them, the Holy Spirit came to them (Acts 19:1-7). Without these experiences, the Jews would never have believed that the baptism of the Holy Spirit was extended to the believers outside the Jews, the chosen people of God.

We are now living after these Pentecostal events, like the 3,000 souls who were converted and baptized that same day, but who never experienced the same miraculous events that had taken place earlier (Acts 2:38-41). There were no sounds from Heaven and no rushing of mighty winds. There were no flames or tongues like fire as on the day of Pentecost (Acts 2:2-4).

When Paul was converted and baptized, he was filled with Holy Spirit, but the Bible does not indicate that he immediately spoke in tongues. The Bible says:

So Ananias went over and found Paul and laid his hands on him and said, "Brother Paul, the Lord Jesus, who appeared to you on the road, has sent me so that you may be filled with the Holy Spirit and get your sight back."

Instantly (it was as though scales fell from his eyes) Paul could see, and was immediately baptized.

Then he ate and was strengthened. (Acts 9:17-19 TLB)

Paul was a linguist; he spoke many languages. He preached in Hebrew, Greek, Latin, Arabic and many other languages of Asia. He was a missionary and learned their languages. Paul said: "I thank God, I speak in tongues more than you all" (1 Cor. 14:18 NAS). That means he spoke languages more than all of them. Paul also said: "Now I wish that you all spoke in tongues..." (1 Cor. 14:5 NAS). Paul did not say that all believers must speak in tongues. He only wished that they all would speak in tongues.

2. Confession

Confess or tell others with your mouth that Jesus Christ is your Lord and Savior, believe in your heart that God raised Him from the dead, and you will be saved. The Bible states the fact that confession is made because you are saved.

> *That if thou shalt confess with thy mouth the Lord Jesus, and shalt believe in thine heart that God hath raised Him from the dead, thou shalt be saved.*
>
> *For with the heart man believeth unto righteousness; and with the mouth confession is made unto salvation.* (Rom. 10:9,10)

Confess Jesus Christ before men. Say that He is your Lord and Savior and He will also confess you before His Father in Heaven. The Bible says:

> *Whosoever therefore shall confess Me before men, him will I confess also before My Father which is in heaven.*
>
> *But whosoever shall deny Me before men, him will I also deny before My Father which is in heaven.* (Matt. 10:32,33)

Chapter IX

Dealing With the Prospects

Born again Christians, as soul winners, must equip themselves with the whole armor of God, the Bible truths, and the sword of the Spirit, which is the Word of God, in dealing with lost souls. A prospect can be converted by the Word of God through the power of the Holy Spirit and with the help of the soul winners who as His instruments, lead him to faith in Jesus Christ as his personal Lord and Savior.

Section A: How to Deal With Prospects Who Are Interested About the Salvation of Their Souls, But Don't Know the Way

There are so many people who are interested in the salvation of their souls, but who don't know the way.

An example is the Ethiopian eunuch. He traveled a long way from Ethiopia to Jerusalem to find salvation, but he started home empty-handed. He didn't know the way to eternal life. He was still searching for the way to everlasting life on his way home. He was reading the Scriptures, but could not understand them. Philip asked the eunuch if he understood what he was reading. "And he said, How can I, except some man should guide me?" (Acts 8:31). With Philip, who guided him, the eunuch found salvation and as proof, he submitted himself to baptism in obedience to the Lord's command.

Without the Holy Spirit who convicted and converted, and the guidance of Philip, the Ethiopian eunuch could have been lost forever.

Another example is the rich young ruler of the Jews. He claimed to have kept the Ten Commndments since he was young. He asked Jesus what he should do to inherit eternal life. When Jesus told him to sell all he had and give to the poor and he would have treasure in Heaven, the young ruler went away sorrowful (Luke 18:18-23).

Now, show the prospect that there are several steps to God's way of salvation. They are the following:

1. Believe

A jailer was in trouble. Trembling with fear, he tried to kill himself. But Paul and Silas, who were among the prisoners, yelled at the jailer not to kill himself. The jailer realized his need of salvation, so he asked, "Sirs, what must I do to be saved?" Paul and Silas answered and said, "Believe on the Lord Jesus Christ, and thou shalt be saved, and thy house" (Acts 16:30,31).

Dealing With the Prospects

"What must I do to be saved?" is the most important question confronting sinners right now. Any prospect who has realized his need of salvation is the easiest one to win and to lead to a new life with Jesus as his personal Lord and Savior.

Remember, the moment you truly believed in Jesus Christ as your personal Lord and Savior, you were saved.

a. Show the prospect that God loved us so much, He gave His only Son that if we would believe in Him, we would have everlasting life. Let him read John 3:16 with you.

For God so loved the world, that He gave His only begotten Son, that whosoever believeth in Him should not perish, but have everlasting life. (John 3:16)

b. Show the prospect that if he believes in Jesus Christ, he will not be condemned, and if he does not believe, he is condemned already. Let the prospect read John 3:18 with you.

He that believeth on Him is not condemned: but he that believed not is condemned already, because he hath not believed in the name of the only begotten Son of God. (John 3:18)

c. Show the prospect that if he listens to Jesus Christ's message and believes in God the Father who sent Him, he will have everlasting life. He will not come into the judgment of God for his sins because he has already passed from death to life. Let the prospect read John 5:24 with you.

Verily, verily, I say unto you, He that heareth My word, and believeth on Him that sent Me, hath everlasting life, and shall not come into condemnation; but is passed from death unto life. (John 5:24)

d. Show the prospect that salvation is a free gift from God and that it is given only to those who have faith in Jesus Christ. He cannot work for it, neither can he purchase it. It is a gift from God through faith. Let the prospect read Ephesians 2:8 and 9 with you.

For by grace are ye saved through faith; and that not of yourselves: it is the gift of God:

Not of works, lest any man should boast. (Eph. 2:8,9)

Read Titus 3:5 also.

e. Show the prospect that he can be justified only by faith and that he cannot be justified by works. Let the prospect read Galatians 2:16 with you.

Knowing that a man is not justified by the works of the law, but by the faith of Jesus Christ, even we have believed in Jesus Christ, that we might be justified by the faith of Christ, and not by the works of the law: for by the works of the law shall no flesh be justified. (Gal. 2:16)

f. Now ask the prospect what he must do to be saved according to the Bible. Go back to Acts 16 and let him read verse 31. Now ask the prospect: "Do you believe now that you need to be saved?"

2. Receive

To truly believe that Jesus Christ is the Son of God and the Lord and Savior, one also must receive Him and invite Him into his heart.

a. Show the prospect that even satan believed, but that he was in terror because he is a liar and a murderer. Let the prospect read James 2:19 with you.

Thou believest that there is one God; thou doest well: the devils also believe, and tremble. (James 2:19)

Let him read John 8:44 with you also.

Ye are of your father the devil, and the lusts of your father ye will do. He was a murderer from the beginning, and abode not in the truth, because there is no truth in him. When he speaketh a lie, he speaketh of his own: for he is a liar, and the father of it. (John 8:44)

b. Show the prospect that he also must receive Christ Jesus in order to become a child of God. Let the prospect read John 1:12 with you.

But as many as received Him, to them gave He power to become the sons of God, even to them that believe on His name. (John 1:12)

c. Show the prospect that he must open the door of his heart and invite Jesus Christ to come into his heart so he can fellowship with Him. Let the prospect read Revelation 3:20 with you.

Behold, I stand at the door, and knock: if any man hear My voice, and open the door, I will come in to him, and will sup with him, and he with Me. (Rev. 3:20)

3. Repent

Although a person's sins are automatically forgiven upon believing and receiving Jesus Christ as his personal

Lord and Savior, he also must acknowledge his sins. One doesn't really believe and receive Him if he doesn't repent from his sins.

a. Show the prospect that once he truly believes and accepts Jesus Christ as his personal Lord and Savior, he has been saved and his sins are forgiven. He also is justified by his faith. Let him read Acts 10:43 with you.

To Him give all the prophets witness, that through His name whosoever believeth in Him shall receive remission of sins. (Acts 10:43)

Therefore we conclude that a man is justified by faith without the deeds of the law. (Rom. 3:28)

Knowing that a man is not justified by the works of the law, but by the faith of Jesus Christ, even we have believed in Jesus Christ, that we might be justified by the faith of Christ, and not by the works of the law: for by the works of the law shall no flesh justified. (Gal. 2:16)

b. Show the prospect that he also must repent from his sins and be willing to start a new life with Jesus Christ, so he will not perish. Let the prospect read Luke 13:3 with you.

I tell you, Nay: but, except ye repent, ye shall all likewise perish. (Luke 13:3)

Then ask the prospect: "Do you now believe and receive Jesus Christ as your Lord and Savior? And repent from your sins?" If the answer is positive, lead him in prayer. Let him repeat, after you, the following prayer.

Lord Jesus Christ, I now believe and accept You as my Lord and Savior. I ask You now to forgive me of my sins. I now open my heart and invite You to come in and live in my heart. Be merciful to me, a sinner. In Jesus' name I pray. Amen.

At this point, you pray for the prospect, that he continue to grow to Christian maturity with the guidance of the Holy Spirit and that he live according to the will of God.

If the prospect really believed from his heart, he is now saved. He now has the assurance of salvation. He now experiences the joy of His salvation.

4. The Manifestations of Salvation

a. Baptism

Jesus Christ commissioned His disciples to go and make disciples, baptizing them in the name of God the Father, God the Son, and God the Holy Spirit; then teaching them to obey all the commands of the Lord. Jesus said:

"I have been given all authority in heaven and earth.

Therefore go and make disciples in all the nations, baptizing them into the name of the Father and of the Son and of the Holy Spirit,

and then teach these new disciples to obey all the commands I have given you; and be sure of this–that I am with you always, even to the end of the world." (Matt. 28:18-20 TLB)

a) Christian Baptism. What is Christian baptism? Christian baptism is a ceremony or rite administered to the new believer to show that he has been saved, for he was justified by his faith. Christian baptism, therefore, is the symbol of spiritual washing, cleansing or purifying.

Show the new believer the different interpretations of the word *baptism*. The dictionary tells us first about the mode of baptism practiced by the different Christian churches, which are dipping in water and sprinkling or pouring water; second, it tells us about the meaning of baptism as the symbol of washing away sins or of spiritual purification. It says baptism is:

> The ceremony or sacrament of admitting a person into Christianity or a specific Christian church by dipping him in water or sprinkling water on him, as a symbol of washing away sin and of spiritual purification (*Webster's New World Dictionary*).

There are those who believe that the word *baptism* means "immersion." To prove this idea, they claim that the root word of "to baptize" is the Greek *bapto* or *baptizo*, meaning "to dip." From this interpretation, they conclude that the meaning of baptism is dipping or immersion (Berkhof 1941:629).

Show the new believer that the words *bapto* or *baptizo* was used four times in the New Testament. Once in Luke, once in Revelation and twice in John. Let the new believer read Luke 16:24 with you:

> *And he cried and said, Father Abraham, have mercy on me, and send Lazarus, that he may **dip** the tip of*

his finger in water, and cool my tongue; for I am tormented in this flame. (Luke 16:24)

And He was clothed with a vesture dipped in blood: and His name is called The Word of God. (Rev. 19:13)

Jesus answered, He it is, to whom I shall give a sop, when I have dipped it. And when He had dipped the sop, He gave it to Judas Iscariot, the son of Simon. (John 13:26)

In all these verses the word *bapto* or *baptizo*, meaning "to dip," do not refer to Christian baptism.

Tell the new believer that there are also those who believe that baptism is the symbol of spiritual purification or cleansing. To prove this belief, they also refer to the Bible. Let the new believer read Acts 22:16 with you.

And now why tarriest thou? arise, and be baptized, and wash away thy sins, calling on the name of the Lord. (Acts 22:16)

Let us draw near with a true heart in full assurance of faith, having our hearts sprinkled from an evil conscience, and our bodies washed with pure water. (Heb. 10:22)

Know ye not, that so many of us as were baptized into Jesus Christ were baptized into His death?

Therefore we are buried with Him by baptism into death: that like as Christ was raised up from the dead by the glory of the Father, even so we also should walk in newness of life. (Rom. 6:3,4)

And such were some of you: but ye are washed, but ye are sanctified, but ye are justified in the name of the Lord Jesus, and by the Spirit of our God. (I Cor. 6:11)

Not by works of righteousness which we have done, but according to His mercy He saved us, by the washing of regeneration, and renewing of the Holy Ghost. (Titus 3:5)

Regarding the mode of baptism, Dr. Berkhof states: The generally prevailing opinion outside the Baptist circle is that, as long as the fundamental idea, namely, that of purification, finds expression in the rite, the mode of baptism is quite immaterial. It may be administered by immersion, by pouring or by effusion, or by sprinkling. The Bible simply uses a generic word to denote an action designed to produce a certain effect, namely, cleansing or purification, but nowhere determines the specific mode in which the effect is to be produced. Jesus did not prescribe a certain mode of baptism (1959:629).

Now, remind the new believer that as soon as a person believes and accepts Jesus Christ as His personal Lord and Savior, he is saved. But he must obey the command of the Lord to be baptized. So the new believer will undergo the rite of baptism not to save himself, but to publicly show that he has been saved already. Baptism, therefore, is an act of the believer in obedience to the command of Jesus Christ.

The Bible has several examples of people who were baptized immediately after conversion. They include the following:

1) The baptism of the Philippian jailer. After his conversion, he and his family were baptized immediately. Let the new believer read Acts 16:32-34 with you.

And they spake unto him the word of the Lord, and to all that were in his house.

And he took them the same hour of the night, and washed their stripes; and was baptized, he and all his, straightway.

And when he had brought them into his house, he set meat before them, and rejoiced, believing in God with all his house. (Acts 16:32-34)

2) The baptism of Cornelius and his family, relatives and friends. After their conversion, they too were baptized immediately. Let the new believer read Acts 10:47 and 48 with you.

Can any man forbid water, that these should not be baptized, which have received the Holy Ghost as well as we?

And he commanded them to be baptized in the name of the Lord.... (Acts 10:47,48)

3) The baptism of Paul. Paul's conversion was a miraculous experience in his life. Show the beliver that Jesus Christ Himself convicted and converted Paul on his way to Damascus. Jesus Christ later instructed Ananias to lay his hands on Paul so he could see again. Let the new believer read Acts 9:17-19 in The Living Bible with you.

So Ananias went over and found Paul and laid his hands on him and said, "Brother Paul, the Lord Jesus, who appeared to you on the road, has sent me so that you may be filled with the Holy Spirit and get your sight back."

Instantly (it was as though scales fell from his eyes) Paul could see, and was immediately baptized.

Then he ate and was strengthened.... (Acts 9:17-19)

Remind the new believer that those references show all were baptized immediately inside the house where they were. There was never any indication that they left the house to be baptized in a river.

4) The baptism of the Ethiopian eunuch. The Ethiopian eunuch was a very religious man. He was on his way home to Ethiopia from Jerusalem, where he had worshiped in the Temple. Show the new believer that the Holy Spirit used Philip as an instrument in leading the Ethiopian eunuch to Jesus Christ as his personal Lord and Savior and that he too was baptized immediately.

Let the new believer read Acts 8:35-38 with you.

Then Philip opened his mouth, and began at the same scripture, and preached unto him Jesus.

And as they went on their way, they came unto a certain water: and the eunuch said, See, here is water; what doth hinder me to be baptized?

And Philip said, If thou believest with all thine heart, thou mayest. And he answered and said, I believe that Jesus Christ is the Son of God.

And he commanded the chariot to stand still: and they went down both into the water, both Philip and the eunuch; and he baptized him. (Acts 8:35-38)

Call the attention of the new believer to the fact that the eunuch was baptized immediately. In this instance, it does not necessarily mean that the eunuch was immersed. In the words of Dr. Berkhof: "Acts 8:36-38, which is often regarded as the strongest Scriptural proof for baptism by immersion, cannot be regarded as conclusive evidence" (1959:630).

Now ask the new believer if he is ready to be baptized publicly in obedience to Jesus' command. If the answer is positive, lead him to be baptized in the Church. Invite him to publicly show that he has been saved.

b. Baptism of the Holy Spirit. In order for the new believer not to be confused by the different interpretations of the baptism of the Holy Spirit, show him that the baptism of the Holy Spirit takes place as soon as the person truly believes and receives Jesus Christ as his personal Lord and Savior.

Remind the new believer that he has been baptized with the Holy Spirit since his conversion. Let him read First Corinthians 12:12 and 13 in The Living Bible with you.

> *Our bodies have many parts, but the many parts make up only one body when they are put together. So it is with the "body" of Christ.*
>
> *Each of us is a part of the one body of Christ. Some of us are Jews, some are Gentiles, some are slaves and some are free. But the Holy Spirit has fitted us all together into one body. We have been baptized into Christ's body by the one Spirit, and have all been given that same Holy Spirit.* (1 Cor. 12:12,13)

From these verses, we come to understand that the baptism of the Holy Spirit is a collective operation of the Holy Spirit, which includes every true believer or born again Christian.

1) Show the new believer that the baptism of the Holy Spirit is different from being filled with the Holy Spirit. There were those who were baptized with the Holy Spirit, but who were never filled with the Holy Spirit. However, there were those who were baptized with the Holy Spirit and were filled with the Holy Spirit at the same time. Those who were filled with the Holy Spirit were controlled by the Holy Spirit. Let the new believer read Ephesians 5:15-18 in The Living Bible with you.

So be careful how you act; these are difficult days. Don't be fools; be wise: make the most of every opportunity you have for doing good.

Don't act thoughtlessly, but try to find out and do whatever the Lord wants you to.

Don't drink too much wine, for many evils lie along that path; be filled instead with the Holy Spirit, and controlled by Him. (Eph. 5:15-18)

This is a comparison of two forces that can control a person. He is controlled either by the Holy Spirit or by the devil.

2) Show the new convert that when a person is filled with wine, he will be controlled and dominated by the wine. Then he acts in an unnatural manner that is evil (Acts 2:13).

However, if a person is filled with the Holy Spirit, he will be controlled and dominated by the Holy Spirit. Then he acts in an unnatural manner that is good (Eph. 5:19).

We have been commanded to be filled with the Holy Spirit, but we were never commanded to be baptized with the Holy Spirit.

3) Show the new believer that Paul was baptized with the Holy Spirit and simultaneously filled with the Holy Spirit (Acts 9:17). We must remember that it is the will of God that all of us be filled with the Holy Spirit. He has also commanded us to be filled with the Holy Spirit. But He will not force us. If we ask, He will give to us. Let the new believer read Luke 11:13 with you.

If ye then, being evil, know how to give good gifts unto your children: how much more shall your heavenly Father give the Holy Spirit to them that ask Him? (Luke 11:13)

In order to be filled with the Holy Spirit, one must be right with God, seeking to do His will.

2. Confession

When a believer publicly confesses Jesus Christ before men, he shows that he has been saved. Jesus Christ promised the believer that He, in turn, would confess him before His Father in Heaven.

a) Show the new convert that, as a believer, he must confess Jesus publicly before men so that Jesus Christ will confess him before God. Let him read Matthew 10:32 and 33 with you.

Whosoever therefore shall confess Me before men, him will I confess also before My Father which is in heaven.

But whosoever shall deny Me before men, him will I also deny before My Father which is in heaven. (Matt. 10:32,33)

b) Show the believer that when confession is made, it must come from the heart through the mouth. Then it shows salvation. It is a fact of which we should not be ashamed. Let the new convert read Romans 10:9-11 with you.

That if thou shalt confess with thy mouth the Lord Jesus, and shalt believe in thine heart that God hath raised Him from the dead, thou shalt be saved.

For with the heart man believeth unto righteousness; and with the mouth confession is made unto salvation.

For the scripture saith, Whosoever believeth on Him shall not be ashamed. (Rom. 10:9-10)

Now help the new convert not to be ashamed, but to confess Jesus Christ and to witness for Him, come what may. Continue to nurture him, helping him witness by using the first and second chapters of this book.

However, if the new convert's growth is slow, nurture him to spiritual maturity by using Part Three of this book.

Section B: How to Deal With the Prospect Who Is Not Concerned About the Salvation of His Soul

Snatch Him From the Flames of Fire

When a prospect is not concerned about the salvation of his soul, when he says that he is not bothered about where God will send him after he dies then scare him until you can snatch him from the flames of fire. Help him and lead him to faith in Jesus Christ. The Bible says in Jude 22 and 23:

And of some have compassion, making a difference.

And others save with fear, pulling them out of the fire; hating even the garment spotted by the flesh. (Jude 22,23)

These verses mean that when a person is interested or concerned about the salvation of his soul, but doesn't know the way, the Bible says to "have compassion" with him and lead him to faith in Jesus Christ. But of the unconcerned, the Bible says to, "save with fear, pulling them out of the fire." However, you must be careful, for you also might be pulled along by their sins. Hate their sins, but be merciful to them as sinners.

1. Show the prospect that if he dies now, he will go to hell, the lake of fire, to be tormented eternally. Let him read Revelation 20:10 with you.

And the devil that deceived them was cast into the lake of fire and brimstone, where the beast and the false prophet are, and shall be tormented day and night for ever and ever. (Rev. 20:10)

And death and hell were cast into the lake of fire. This is the second death.

And whosoever was not found written in the book of life was cast into the lake of fire (Rev. 20:14,15).

The prospect might say he is not evil enough to be tormented in the lake of fire.

2. Show the prospect that all have sinned, including yourself. Let him read Romans 3:23 with you.

For all have sinned, and come short of the glory of God. (Rom. 3:23)

3. Now remind the prospect that, according to the Bible, he is a sinner before God. He might say that he

did not commit any crime or sin. Let him read First John 1:8 and 10 with you.

If we say that we have no sin, we deceive ourselves, and the truth is not in us.

If we say that we have not sinned, we make Him a liar, and His word is not in us. (I John 1:8,10)

4. Show the prospect that the wages of sin is death. It is the second death that was mentioned in Revelation 20:14. It says: "And death and hell were cast into the lake of fire. This is the second death." Let him read Romans 6:23 with you.

For the wages of sin is death; but the gift of God is eternal life through Jesus Christ our Lord. (Rom. 6:23)

5. Show the prospect that death means eternal punishment in the lake of fire. Let him read Revelation 21:8 with you.

But cowards who turn back from following Me, and those who are unfaithful to Me, and the corrupt, and murderers, and the immoral, and those conversing with demons, and idol worshipers and all liars—their doom is in the Lake that burns with fire and sulphur. This is the Second Death. (Rev. 21:8 TLB)

Lead Him to Faith in Jesus Christ

Confront the prospect and ask him if he wants to spend eternity in the lake that burns with fire. At this point, the prospect might be scared and ask for help. He might say, "What must I do to be saved?"

1. Show the prospect that he must believe in Jesus Christ as his personal Lord and Savior to be saved. Let him read Acts 16:30 and 31 with you.

And brought them out, and said, Sirs, what must I do to be saved?

And they said, Believe on the Lord Jesus Christ, and thou shalt be saved, and thy house. (Acts 16:30,31)

This is God's plan of salvation. He gave us a gift. If we believe and receive the gift, He will redeem us from death to life. Now let the prospect read John 3:16 with you.

For God so loved the world, that He gave His only begotten Son, that whosoever believeth in Him should not perish, but have everlasting life. (John 3:16b)

2. Show the prospect that if he will not believe, he is already condemned. Let him read John 3:18 with you.

He that believeth on Him is not condemned: but he that believeth not is condemned already, because he hath not believed in the name of the only begotten Son of God. (John 3:18)

Have compassion and lead him to faith in Jesus Christ as his personal Lord and Savior by using section A of this chapter.

Section C: How to Deal With the Prospect Who Claims to Be Righteous

The Righteous Man

This class of people claims to be righteous because they are good citizens of the community and observe the golden rules. They claim that they have not violated any law of either government or God. They claim that they are honest, pay their obligations to the government and give donations to charity and to the needy. There are no records whatsoever that stain their reputation. Based upon these concepts, they claim to be righteous and hope to go to Heaven with God.

1. Show the prospect that such righteousness will not save him, for it will fade away. Let him read Isaiah 64:6 with you.

But we are all as an unclean thing, and all our righteousness are as filthy rags; and we all do fade as a leaf... (Isa. 64:6)

Not by works of righteousness which we have done, but according to His mercy He saved us, by the washing of regeneration, and renewing of the Holy Ghost. (Titus 3:5)

2. Show the prospect that the observance of the law has nothing to do with salvation. Let him read Romans 3:20 with you.

Therefore by the deeds of the law there shall no flesh be justified in His sight: for by the law is the knowledge of sin. (Rom. 3:20)

I am not one of those who treats Christ's death as meaningless. For if we could be saved by keeping the Jewish laws, then there was no need for Christ to die. (Gal. 2:21 TLB)

3. Show the prospect that no one is righteous before God; we are all sinners in His sight. Let him read Romans 3:10 and 23 with you.

As it is written, There is none righteous, no, not one.

For all have sinned, and come short of the glory of God. (Rom. 3:10,23)

4. Show the prospect that the wages of sin is death, the second death stated in Revelation. Let him read Romans 6:23 with you.

For the wages of sin is death; but the gift of God is eternal life through Jesus Christ our Lord. (Rom. 6:23)

5. Show the prospect that death is eternal punishment in the lake of fire. Let him read Revelation 20:14 and 21:8 with you.

And death and hell were cast into the lake of fire. This is the second death. (Rev. 20:14)

But the fearful, and unbelieving, and the abominable, and murderers, and whoremongers, and sorcerers, and idolaters, and all liars, shall have their part in the lake which burneth with fire and brimstone: which is the second death. (Rev. 21:8)

Lead Him to Faith in Jesus Christ

Now confront the prospect and ask him if he wants to spend eternity suffering in the lake of fire. By this time, he might be scared and ask for help. Lead him to faith in Jesus Christ as his personal Lord and Savior by using section A of this chapter.

Section D: How to Deal With the Prospect Who Claims to Be Religious

The Religious Man

These people claim to be Christians and, as Christians, they are religious because they observe the Ten Commandments. They pray to God every day, go to church twice a week, regularly give offerings to the church and give donations to charity and the needy. Based on this concept, they hope to go to Heaven.

1. Show the prospect that Cornelius was a very religious man. He worshiped the Lord, prayed to God always and gave donations to charity and to the needy. Let him read Acts 10:1 and 2 with you.

There was a certain man in Caesarea called Cornelius, a centurion of the band called the Italian band.

A devout man, and one that feared God with all his house, which gave much alms to the people, and prayed to God alway. (Acts 10:1,2)

2. Show the prospect that Cornelius was a very religious man, but that he was lost. Let him read Acts 10:5 and 6 and 11:14 with you.

And now send men to Joppa, and call for one Simon, whose name is Peter:

He lodgeth with one Simon a tanner, whose house is by the sea side: he shall tell thee what thou oughtest to do. (Acts 10:5,6)

Who shall tell the words, whereby thou and all thy house shall be saved. (Acts 11:14)

Peter still will tell Cornelius how he and his household can be saved.

3. Show the prospect that not all who say: "Lord, Lord," will enter the Kingdom of God. Let him read Matthew 7:21 with you.

Not every one that saith unto Me, Lord, Lord, shall enter into the kingdom of heaven; but he that doeth the will of My Father which is in heaven. (Matt. 7:21)

4. Show the prospect that all are sinners; you first, then him. Let him read Romans 3:23 with you.

For all have sinned, and come short of the glory of God. (Rom. 3:23)

5. Show the prospect that death means eternal suffering in the lake of fire. Let him read Revelation 20:14 and 21:8 with you.

And death and hell were cast into the lake of fire. This is the second death. (Rev. 20:14)

But the fearful, and unbelieving, and the abominable, and murderers, and whoremongers, and sorcerers, and idolaters, and all liars, shall have their part in the lake which burneth with fire and brimstone: which is the second death. (Rev. 21:8)

Lead Him to Faith in Jesus Christ

1. Remind the righteous man that he will go to hell if he does not change his course. At this point he might be scared and ask you to help him to be saved. Lead him to faith in Jesus Christ by using Section A of this chapter.

2. Show the prospect, if he is not yet convinced, that he will be likened to the rich young ruler of the Jews. That young man was by the door to Heaven, but lost. He told Jesus that he had obeyed all the laws since he was a small child, but when Jesus told him to go and sell all he had and give to the poor, so he would have treasure in Heaven, he went away sorrowful. Let the prospect read Luke 18:21-23 with you.

And he said, All these have I kept from my youth up.

Now when Jesus heard these things, He said unto him, Yet lackest thou one thing: sell all that thou hast, and distribute unto the poor, and thou shalt have treasure in heaven: and come, follow Me.

And when he heard this, he was very sorrowful: for he was very rich. (Luke 18:21-23)

By this time the prospect might have changed his mind and asked for help. Lead him to faith in Jesus Christ as his personal Lord and Savior by using Section A of this chapter.

To accomplish all these things, the soul winner must always be alert, and planning ahead, to present Jesus Christ to the prospects. In so doing, you are planting the seeds of faith that will eventually bring forth much fruit. Soul winners must not only have courage and the boldness of the prophets of old, but also have compassion and understanding, and be loving, humble, kind, wise, and courteous.

NOTE: There are many groups or sects that are misguided by their erroneous views of the Scriptures. But only the major sects are included in this book. They include the following: the Roman Catholics (Romano Catolico); the Philippine Independent Church; the Church of Jesus Christ of the Latter Day Saints; the Seventh Day Adventist Church; the Jehovah's Witnesses; and the Iglesia ni Cristo (Manalo). For guidance on dealing with prospects of these specific sects, refer to the Appendices at the end of this book.

Chapter X

Dealing With the Prospects in General

This chapter is specially designed to help the born again Christians who have been trained, but who have no experience in soul winning. Even if they are still familiarizing themselves with the Scriptures, they can use this chapter as a tool when dealing with prospects, regardless of the prospects' background—religious or secular. The soul winner may win any lost soul with confidence, even though he cannot memorize a single Bible verse, by using this chapter.

Most believers are reluctant to win lost souls to Jesus Christ as their personal Lord and Savior because of fear. They don't know what to say or what to do. Fear is the primary drawback to soul winning. Fear is the main weapon the devil uses to keep the new soul winner from soul winning.

This chapter is a tool for new, unexperienced soul winners. It will give them the confidence and the boldness they need to win lost souls. This process will end in success when they follow it. The more they keep on trying, the greater the results it will produce.

The Preparation

The materials needed in drawing up the plan of soul winning include the following: a marker, a fine point ball pen and a Bible. I recommend using a New Testament, pocket size. Once you have those items, we are ready to draw up the plan of soul winning.

In the inside of the front or back cover of your Bible, write: The Way to Soul Winning. Under this title, write: 2 Timothy 3:16. Also write the page if you are not familiar with the books, chapters and verses of the Bible.

Now open your Bible to Second Timothy 3:16 and mark it with your marker. In any space beside verse 16, or in the margin, write with your pen: Romans 3:23.

Turn to Romans 3:23 and mark it with your marker. Beside verse 23, write: Romans 6:23.

Open your Bible to Romans 6:23 and mark it with your marker. Beside verse 23, write: Revelation 21:8.

Continue the same process in your Bible with the following references: Revelation 21:8; John 3:16;

Dealing With the Prospects in General

Ephesians 2:8,9; John 1:12; Revelation 3:20; 2 Corinthians 6:2; John 14:6; Acts 4:12; Acts 16:31; John 3:18; John 3:36; John 5:24; John 6:40; John 6:47; Acts 10:43; Acts 13:39; and start all over again in John 3:16.

The Layout

List your prospects, as previously stated in Chapter VII. Begin with the unsaved members of your family, if there are any. They are your first priority. Next are your other relatives, then your friends. Then concentrate on others, wherever you find them through the leading of the Holy Spirit.

Pray for your prospects every day. Pray that God will prepare the way. You need to have a schedule. You should have a definite time of the day to pray for your prospects and a definite time of the day to go out soul winning. Start your soul winning with one or two from the top of your list. Pause for a moment and breathe a word of prayer before you go out soul winning, for without God, you cannot do anything. If you go out with a partner, pray with him. It is the Holy Spirit who convicts and converts the lost souls. You are only an instrument to win them to Jesus Christ.

If you are going out in teams, the husband and wife team is the best. When in teams, decide who among you will do the talking. The other partner will clear the way so no one can interrupt the process. If the prospect is in the home, the partner will answer the telephone or the door, telling the callers that the prospect is busy right now and unable to answer the call. The partner could tell them to try again in an hour or two. If a child is bothering the prospect, the partner will do the baby sitting. The partner will also assist the prospect in finding the Bible references, so the prospect will feel comfortable. Remember, the one who is doing the talking is in control. Do not allow the prospect to control the process. If he asks questions, tell him that his questions are good and that you will note them and deal with them after you are finished with God's plan of salvation.

The Act

After a pleasant exchange of greetings with the prospect, always be alert to look for an opening to ask him the first question. If you have an opening, ask him: "Do you know where you will go when you leave this world?" Or ask: "Do you know where you will go if you die tonight?" The most common answers are the following: "I don't know," "I am not sure," and "To Heaven, I hope." A lost person, because of ignorance, will seldom say "To Heaven." If he does, ask him, "How do you know that you will go to Heaven?" You will know by his answers that he is lost. The only person who is sure of going to Heaven is the one who is a truly born again Christian, who truly believed and received Jesus Christ as his personal Lord and Savior. If you encounter a true Christian, congratulate him and encourage him to keep on believing and to keep on doing God's will. Say good-bye and leave. Do not convert those who have already been converted. That means, do not proselytize. Go to your next prospect.

The next question you want to ask is this: "Do you want to know for sure how can you go to Heaven when you die?" If he does, the follow-up question is this: "Do you believe that the Bible is inspired of God?" Prove to him that the Scripture is inspired of God by opening your Bible and letting him read Second Timothy 3:16 with you:

All scripture is given by inspiration of God, and is profitable for doctrine, for reproof, for correction, for instruction in righteousness. (II Tim. 3:16)

If the prospect believes that the Bible is inspired of God, ask him the next question: "If I can show you how you can go to Heaven, according to the Bible, are you willing to do what the Bible says?" While you are still talking, turn your Bible to Romans 3:23. Tell him that according to the Bible, everybody is a sinner. That means, you yourself are a sinner, the prospect is a sinner and everyone is a sinner. Now let him read Romans 3:23 with you.

For all have sinned, and come short of the glory of God. (Rom. 3:23)

(Read also Romans 3:10.)

Then ask: "Do you now believe that everybody is a sinner, including you?" Have him agree that he is a sinner according to the Bible. While you are still talking, turn your Bible to Romans 6:23.

Show the prospect that the wages of sin is death which is the second death. Let him read Romans 6:23 with you.

For the wages of sin is death; but the gift of God is eternal life through Jesus Christ our Lord. (Rom. 6:23)

Show the prospect that, since everybody is a sinner, everybody will go to hell and to the lake of fire to be tormented eternally. Let him read Revelation 21:8 with you.

But the fearful, and unbelieving, and the abominable, and murderers, and whoremongers, and sorcerers, and idolaters, and all liars, shall have their part in the lake which burneth with fire and brimstone: which is the second death. (Rev. 21:8)

Now ask the prospect if he wants to go to the lake of fire to be tormented eternally. Of course he will say no. Nobody wants to go to hell or to the lake of fire and be tormented eternally.

Show the prospect that God has a plan for the salvation of all, so all may have eternal life. Let him read John 3:16 with you.

For God so loved the world, that He gave His only begotten Son, that whosoever believeth in Him should not perish, but have everlasting life. (John 3:16)

Show the prospect that salvation is a gift from God to those who believe on Him. A person cannot work for it; neither can one buy it. Let him read Ephesians 2:8 and 9 with you.

For by grace are ye saved through faith; and that not of yourselves: it is the gift of God:

Not of works, lest any man should boast. (Eph. 2:8,9)

Now ask the prospect: "Do you want to be saved and have everlasting life?" If the answer is positive, ask him the following question: "What does the Bible say for you to do to have eternal life?" The Bible says: "Whosoever believeth in Him should not perish, but have everlasting life." "For by grace are ye saved through faith...it is the gift of God."

Then ask the prospect: "Do you now believe in Jesus Christ as your personal Lord and Savior?" If the answer is positive, he is saved, but he still needs to receive Him to become a son of God.

Show the prospect that if he believes, he must also receive Jesus Christ in order to be called the son of God. Let him read John 1:12 with you.

But as many as received Him, to them gave He power to become the sons of God, even to them that believe on His name. (John 1:12)

Now ask the prospect: "Do you now receive Jesus Christ in your heart, to be the son of God?" If the answer is positive, congratulate him and lead him to pray the sinner's prayer. Ask him to pray with you. "Would you like to pray with me and ask God to forgive you of your sins? We will pray together with bowed heads, closed eyes. Just follow me in this simple prayer; then I will pray for you."

Lord Jesus, I now believe and receive You as my personal Lord and Savior. I know now that I am a sinner. I now confess my sins. I ask You to forgive me of my sins and save my soul. Amen.

Now you, the soul winner, pray for him in this manner, or with your own prayer.

Almighty and everlasting God, our heavenly Father, we thank You for Your transforming power, in the conversion of this brother. We pray that he may understand in his heart that salvation is by faith in Jesus Christ, that eternal life is by believing in Him. Give him the knowledge and wisdom to understand Your Word. Give him the joy and the assurance of Your salvation. In Jesus' most precious name we pray. Amen.

Show the new believer that he can know he has eternal life. Let him read First John 5:13 with you.

These things have I written unto you that believe on the name of the Son of God; that ye may know that ye have eternal life, and that ye may believe on the name of the Son of God. (I John 5:13)

Now invite him to church with you. Pick him up if he doesn't have a ride. Let him sit with you so he will feel comfortable. Help him locate the hymns and the scripture lessons. Introduce him to the pastor, so the pastor can take over for spiritual growth. Your mission is now over as a beginner. However, this is just the *first step*. If the prospect is not yet convinced, move to the second step.

Second Step

Show the prospect that Jesus Christ is knocking at the door of his heart. If he opens the door, Jesus will enter in and reside in his heart to control, to lead and to guide him all the way. Let him read Revelation 3:20 with you.

> *Behold, I stand at the door, and knock: if any man hear My voice, and open the door, I will come in to him, and will sup with him, and he with Me.* (Rev. 3:20)

Ask the prospect if he will now believe, receive and open the door of his heart and let Jesus come in to him. He most likely will. Very few go beyond this second step. If the answer is positive, lead him to pray the sinner's prayer. Ask him to pray with you. "Would you like to pray with me and ask God to forgive you of your sins? Follow me and we will pray together with bowed heads and eyes closed."

> *Lord Jesus, I now believe and receive You as my personal Lord and Savior. I now open my heart and invite You to come into my heart. I acknowledge my sins. I ask You to forgive me of my sins and save my soul. Amen.*

At this time, pray for the new believer. Then invite him to church, even offer to pick him up. Make him comfortable by helping him locate the hymns and scripture lessons. Introduce him to the pastor, so the pastor can take over for spiritual growth. As a beginner, you have accomplished you mission. But if the response is still negative, move to the third step.

Third Step

Show the prospect that today is the accepted time, that now is the day of salvation, for tomorrow might be too late. Tell him that he has nothing to lose if he would believe, open his heart and invite Jesus Christ to come in. If he will not believe and he dies tonight, he would lose everything. Let him read Second Corinthians 6:2 with you.

(For He saith, I have heard thee in a time accepted, and in the day of salvation have I succoured thee: behold, now is the accepted time; behold, now is the day of salvation.) (II Cor. 6:2)

At this stage, the prospect may have a second thought and decide to believe and invite Jesus Christ to come into his heart. Continue the same process as stated in the first step and the second step. If he is not yet persuaded, move to the fourth step.

Fourth Step

Very few, if any, will go beyond this stage. Show the prospect that salvation is given only by faith. If he does not believe, the Bible says he is already condemned. Let him read Acts 16:31 and John 3:18 with you.

And they said, Believe on the Lord Jesus Christ, and thou shalt be saved, and thy house. (Acts 16:31)

He that believeth on Him is not condemned: but he that believeth not is condemned already, because he hath not believed in the name of the only begotten Son of God. (John 3:18)

At this stage the prospect will be scared and ask you for help. You know already the procedure; just continue to follow it.

Dealing With the Prospects in General

Fifth Step

In case there is a prospect who still goes beyond the fourth step, show him that there are many other scriptures to prove that salvation is by faith in Jesus Christ. Let him read the following scriptures with you:

John 14:6

Jesus saith unto him, I am the way, the truth, and the life: no man cometh unto the Father, but by Me.

Acts 4:12

Neither is there salvation in any other: for there is none other name under heaven given among men, whereby we must be saved.

John 3:36

He that believeth on the Son hath everlasting life: and he that believeth not the Son shall not see life; but the wrath of God abideth on him.

John 5:24

Verily, verily, I say unto you, He that heareth My word, and believeth on Him that sent Me, hath everlasting life, and shall not come into condemnation; but is passed from death unto life.

John 6:40

And this is the will of Him that sent Me, that every one which seeth the Son, and believeth on Him, may have everlasting life: and I will raise him up at the last day.

John 6:47

Verily, verily, I say unto you, He that believeth on Me hath everlasting life.

At this stage, the prospect should be convinced. So he believes and asks you for help. You already know what to do. Continue the procedure.

Should there be any prospect who goes beyond this step, which I doubt very much, go back to John 3:16 and start all over again.

Part Three

Discipling

Jesus Christ, our divine Lord and Savior, commissioned His disciples, saying: "Go ye therefore, and teach all nations, baptizing them in the name of the Father, and of the Son, and of the Holy Ghost: teaching them to observe all things whatsoever I have commanded you: and, lo, I am with you alway, even unto the end of the world. Amen" (Matt. 28:19,20).

What is the meaning of discipling? It is the process or act of a true Christian to actually teach, guide and bring the new believer or babe in faith to spiritual maturity in the manifold grace and knowledge of God our Father; of Jesus Christ the Son, our divine Lord and Savior; and of the Holy Spirit, our Guide and our Comforter. That results in spiritual growth and stability.

Chapter XI

Discipling the New Believer to Spiritual Maturity

To help a new believer grow spiritually, the trained soul winner, teacher or minister will guide, teach and lead this babe in faith to spiritual maturity.

Leading the lost person to faith in Jesus Christ as his personal divine Lord and Savior is not the end of your responsibility and ministry. You must help the new believer to truly understand the basic steps in knowing and doing the will of God as a manifestation of spiritual growth.

You need to train the new believer to be faithful and to accept his responsibilities as a child of God so you will not lose what you have accomplished. "Look to yourselves, that we lose not those things which we have wrought, but that we receive a full reward" (II John 8).

Steps to Know the Will of God

When a person has really been saved, many things will happen in his life. For example, he is "redeemed;" he is "bought with a price;" he is "born again;" he is made a "new creature;" he receives a "new life;" he becomes a "Son of God;" etc. But that is not the end. He also must know and understand the perfect will of God as a prerequisite to spiritual maturity. We will undoubtedly know God's perfect will as soon as we choose God's will for our lives.

There are three steps to knowing the perfect will of God, according to the apostle Paul in his letter to the Romans.

1. Present

There are many believers who do not present or consecrate their bodies, their lives, to the service of the Lord. However, there are multitudes of believers who have presented or consecrated themselves to the service of the Lord as a "living sacrifice, holy, acceptable unto God."

Show the new believer that, as a prerequisite to knowing the will of God, he is to surrender or present his body as a "living sacrifice, holy, [and] acceptable unto God." Let him read Romans 12:1 with you.

I beseech you therefore, brethren, by the mercies of God, that ye present your bodies a living sacrifice, holy, acceptable unto God, which is your reasonable service. (Rom. 12:1)

2. Conform

There are many believers who are living a worldly life, conforming to or following the worldly customs. They are called carnal Christians. They could not turn their back on worldliness, or worldy pleasures and desires. However, there are multitudes of believers who are obedient to the will of God, who do turn their backs on worldly customs. They do not conform to or follow the customs of the world, but to the things from above.

Show the new believer that the Bible teaches us not to love the world or worldly things, or in other words, to not conform or follow the worldly customs. If we do, the love of God is not in us. Let him read First John 2:15 with you.

Love not the world, neither the things that are in the world. If any man love the world, the love of the Father is not in him. (I John 2:15)

It is clear that, according to this scripture, Christians should not follow or conform to worldly customs. The Bible says: "And be not conformed to this world" (Rom. 12:2a).

3. Transform

There are many believers whose lives were not transformed or changed to that of spiritual life. However, there are multitudes of believers whose lives were transformed to that of spiritual life, who conformed to God's spiritual frame of mind. Without a real transformation to spiritual life, one will never know the perfect will of God. Let the new believer read Romans 12:2b with you.

But be ye transformed by the renewing of your mind, that ye may prove what is that good, and acceptable, and perfect, will of God. (Rom. 12:2b)

Show the new believer that knowing the "good, and acceptable, and perfect, will of God" is not enough. He must continue to do God's will. Let him read First John 2:17 with you.

And the world passeth away, and the lust thereof: but he that doeth the will of God abideth forever. (I John 2:17)

The Six Steps to Spiritual Maturity

1. Always Abide in Jesus Christ

a. Show the new believer that, as a born again Christian, he must always abide with Jesus Christ in order to grow and bear fruit. Let him read John 15:4-6 with you.

Abide in Me, and I in you. As the branch cannot bear fruit of itself, except it abide in the vine; no more can ye, except ye abide in Me.

I am the vine, ye are the branches: He that abideth in Me, and I in him, the same bringeth forth much fruit: for without Me ye can do nothing.

If a man abide not in Me, he is cast forth as a branch, and is withered; and men gather them, and cast them into the fire, and they are burned. (John 15:4-6)

b. Show the new believer that, as a new babe in faith, he is not immune from temptations. He is like a small baby trying to walk by himself—he will fall many times in his attempts—but who doesn't quit until he has learned how to walk. Likewise, as a new believer or babe in faith, he will be overtaken by sin. That means, in his attempt to walk righteously in Jesus Christ, he will trip on the way. However, he must stand up and return to the fellowship with Jesus Christ. He should ask for forgiveness, and Jesus will gladly forgive him. Let him read First John 1:7 and 9 with you.

But if we walk in the light, as He is in the light, we have fellowship one with another, and the blood of Jesus Christ His Son cleanseth us from all sin.

If we confess our sins, He is faithful and just to forgive us our sins, and to cleanse us from all unrighteousness. (I John 1:7,9)

c. Show the new believer that, if he abides in the teaching of Jesus Christ, he will have both the Father and the Son. Let him read Second John 9 with you.

Whosoever transgresseth, and abideth not in the doctrine of Christ, hath not God. He that abideth in the doctrine of Christ, he hath both the Father and the Son. (II John 9)

2. Always Commune With God in the Reading and Understanding of His Word

a. Show the new believer that the Word of God is food for the soul, to those who are saved or born again Christians. As a small baby in faith, he is to begin a new life, a Christian life, by reading the Bible so he can grow spiritually. Let him read First Peter 2:2 and 3 with you.

As newborn babes, desire the sincere milk of the word, that ye may grow thereby:

If so be ye have tasted that the Lord is gracious. (I Pet. 2:2,3)

b.   Show the new believer that when a person is still a babe in faith and still drinking milk, he doesn't yet know the difference between good and bad. He must learn to eat solid spiritual food so he will be able to understand the deeper words of God, and understand good and bad. Let him read Hebrews 5:13 and 14 with you.

For every one that useth milk is unskillful in the word of righteousness: for he is a babe.

But strong meat belongeth to them that are of full age, even those who by reason of use have their senses exercised to discern both good and evil. (Heb. 5:13,14)

c.   Show the new believer that he will receive a special blessing from God if he reads his Bible regularly. Let him read Revelation 1:3 with you.

Blessed is he that readeth, and they that hear the words of this prophecy, and keep those things which are written therein: for the time is at hand. (Rev. 1:3)

d.   Show the new believer that bread cannot feed the soul, but obedience to the Word of God nourishes it. Let him read Matthew 4:4 with you.

But He answered and said, It is written, Man shall not live by bread alone, but by every word that proceedeth out of the mouth of God. (Matt. 4:4)

e.   Show the new believer that he will grow strong spiritually, in the knowledge of Jesus Christ, his personal divine Lord and Savior. Let him read Second Peter 3:18 with you.

But grow in grace, and in the knowledge of our Lord and Saviour Jesus Christ. To Him be glory both now and for ever. Amen. (II Pet. 3:18)

f. Show the new believer that the precious Word of God will teach him to do what is good and what is right. Let him read Second Timothy 3:16 and 17 with you.

All scripture is given by inspiration of God, and is profitable for doctrine, for reproof, for correction, for instruction in righteousness:

That the man of God may be perfect, throughly furnished unto all good works. (II Tim. 3:16,17)

3. Always Commune With God in Prayer

a. Show the new believer that he must always begin with a prayer in every meditation and reading of His Word. Let him read Psalm 119:18 with you.

Open Thou mine eyes, that I may behold wondrous things out of Thy law. (Ps. 119:18)

b. Show the new believer that he ought to pray three times a day as King David did. Let him read Psalm 55:17 with you.

Evening, and morning, and at noon, will I pray, and cry aloud: and He shall hear my voice. (Ps. 55:17)

c. Show the new believer that even the prophet Daniel prayed three times a day. Let him read Daniel 6:10 with you.

Now when Daniel knew that the writing was signed, he went into his house; and his windows being open in his chamber toward Jerusalem, he kneeled upon his knees three times a day, and prayed, and gave thanks before his God as he did aforetime. (Dan. 6:10)

d. Show the new believer that he should praise and thank God continually in prayer. Let him read Hebrews 13:15 with you.

By Him therefore let us offer the sacrifice of praise to God continually, that is, the fruit of our lips giving thanks to His name. (Heb. 13:15)

e. Show the new believer that his prayers are to be made known to God. Let him read Philippians 4:6 with you.

Be careful for nothing; but in every thing by prayer and supplication with thanksgiving let your requests be made known unto God. (Phil. 4:6)

f. Show the new believer that God will hear his prayers if he asks according to His will. Let him read First John 5:14 with you.

And this is the confidence that we have in Him, that, if we ask any thing according to His will, He heareth us. (I John 5:14)

g. Show the new believer that, as a true believer, whatever he asks in prayer, God will answer him. Let him read John 14:11-14 with you.

Believe Me that I am in the Father, and the Father in Me: or else believe Me for the very works' sake.

Verily, verily, I say unto you, He that believeth on Me, the works that I do shall he do also; and greater works than these shall he do; because I go unto My Father.

And whatsoever ye shall ask in My name, that will I do, that the Father may be glorified in the Son.

If ye shall ask any thing in My name, I will do it. (John 14:11-14)

h. Show the new believer that he will get anything he asks for in prayer if he believes. Let him read Matthew 21:22 with you.

And all things, whatsoever ye shall ask in prayer, believing, ye shall receive. (Matt. 21:22)

i. Show the new believer that if he abides with Jesus Christ and obeys His commands, he will ask anything and it will be given to him. Let him read John 15:7 with you.

If ye abide in Me, and My words abide in you, ye shall ask what ye will, and it shall be done unto you. (John 15:7)

j. Show the new believer that his prayers will not be granted if his motives are not right with God. Let him read James 4:3 with you.

Ye ask, and receive not, because ye ask amiss, that ye may consume it upon your lusts. (James 4:3)

Compare this verse with the verse from The Living Bible.

And even when you do ask you don't get it because your whole aim is wrong—you want only what will give you pleasure. (James 4:3 TLB)

4. Always Share Your Experiences With the Lord to Others

One of the greatest miracles in the life of an individual is when he is born again, when he is converted, when his life is changed, when he is born anew, born from above.

His changed life is manifested through his actions and through his words. The Bible says in Matthew 12:34: "...for out of the abundance of the heart the mouth speaketh." Sharing your experiences with others is vital in the growth of Christian life.

a. Show the new believer that, as a true believer, he is ready to glorify the Lord by sharing his hopes with others. Let him read First Peter 3:15 with you.

But sanctify the Lord God in your hearts: and be ready always to give an answer to every man that asketh you a reason of the hope that is in you with meekness and fear. (I Pet. 3:15)

b. Show the new believer that he should be ready to share the goodness of God with others all day long. Let him read Psalm 71:24 with you.

My tongue also shall talk of Thy righteousness all the day long: for they are confounded, for they are brought unto shame, that seek my hurt. (Ps. 71:24)

c. Show the new believer that he should grow in spiritual strength and in the knowledge of the Lord. Let him read Second Peter 3:18 with you.

But grow in grace, and in the knowledge of our Lord and Saviour Jesus Christ. To Him be glory both now and for ever. Amen. (II Pet. 3:18)

d. Show the new believer that he should not be ashamed to share with others what God has done in his life. Let him read Luke 8:39 with you.

Return to thine own house, and shew how great things God hath done unto thee. And he went his way and published throughout the whole city how great things Jesus had done unto him. (Luke 3:39)

e. Show the new believer that he should not be ashamed to share the gospel of Jesus Christ to others. Let him read Romans 1:16 with you.

For I am not ashamed of the gospel of Christ: for it is the power of God unto salvation to every one that believeth... (Rom. 1:16)

f. Show the new believer that those who do not share the good news are often weak in their faith, but that those who share their testimonies grow in grace. Let him Revelation 12:11 with you.

And they overcame him by the blood of the Lamb, and by the word of their testimony; and they loved not their lives unto the death. (Rev. 12:11)

5. Always Fellowship in the Church

To grow in spiritual maturity is the privilege of every true believer who has Jesus Christ as divine Lord and Savior. Those who stop growing spiritually soon die spiritually. That is spiritual death, separation from God. But those who grow continually in grace, will grow to spiritual maturity because they regularly attend church meetings and services that encourage them to actively grow in the service of the Lord.

a. Show the new believer that when he believed and accepted Jesus Christ as his personal and divine Lord and Savior, he became a member of the universal Church, of which Jesus Christ is the Head. Let him read First Corinthians 12:27 with you.

Now you are the body of Christ, and each one of you is a part of it. (I Cor. 12:27 NIV)

b. Show the new believer that he also must be a member of a local church or a local congregation to grow in grace, as it is part of the Church of Jesus Christ, the God who became a man. Let him read Acts 20:28 with you.

*Take heed therefore unto yourselves, and to all the flock, over the which the Holy Ghost hath made you overseers, to feed the **church of God**, which He hath purchased with His own blood.* (Acts 20:28)

c. Show the new believer that he must present his body as a living sacrifice to God, and consecrate his life in the church to be transformed and to know what is good and acceptable to God. Let him read Romans 12:1 and 2 with you.

I beseech you therefore, brethren, by the mercies of God, that ye present your bodies a living sacrifice, holy, acceptable unto God, which is your reasonable service.

And be not conformed to this world: but be ye transformed by the renewing of your mind, that ye may prove what is that good, and acceptable, and perfect, will of God. (Rom. 12:1,2)

d. Show the new believer that, as a true believer, he is the temple of God. Let him read First Corinthians 6:19 and 20 with you.

What? know ye not that your body is the temple of the Holy Ghost which is in you, which ye have of God, and ye are not your own?

For ye are bought with a price: therefore glorify God in your body, and in your spirit, which are God's. (I Cor. 6:19,20)

e. Show the new believer that he must not forget to attend church services in order to grow spiritually. Let him read Hebrews 10:25 with you.

Not forsaking the assembling of ourselves together, as the manner of some is; but exhorting one another: and so much the more, as ye see the day approaching. (Heb. 10:25)

f. Show the new believer that when Jesus Christ was resurrected from the grave on that first day of the week, He commissioned Mary Magdalene and the other Mary to tell His disciples to meet Him in Galilee. Let the new believer read Matthew 28:10 with you.

Then said Jesus unto them, Be not afraid: go tell My brethren that they go into Galilee, and there shall they see Me. (Matt. 28:10)

g. Show the new believer that the disciples worshiped Jesus on that first day of the week in Galilee. Let him read Matthew 28:16 and 17 with you.

Then the eleven disciples went away into Galilee, into a mountain where Jesus had appointed them.

And when they saw Him, they worshipped Him: but some doubted. (Matt. 28:16,17)

h. Show the new believer that on the following Sunday, the first day of the week, the disciples again assembled to worship Jesus. Let him read John 20:26-29 with you.

And after eight days again His disciples were within, and Thomas with them: then came Jesus, the doors being shut, and stood in the midst, and said, Peace be unto you.

Then saith He to Thomas, Reach hither thy finger, and behold My hands; and reach hither thy hand, and thrust it into My side: and be not faithless, but believing.

And Thomas answered and said unto Him, My Lord and my God.

Jesus saith unto him, Thomas, because thou hast seen Me, thou hast believed: blessed are they that have not seen, and yet have believed. (John 20:26-29)

i. Show the new believer that the disciples assembled again on the first day of the week to worship, and Paul preached the Word. Let him read Acts 20:7 with you.

And upon the first day of the week, when the disciples came together to break bread, Paul preached unto them, ready to depart on the morrow; and continued his speech until midnight. (Acts 20:7)

j. Show the new believer that the first church started on Sunday, the first day of the week. Let him read Acts 1:12-14 with you.

> *Then returned they unto Jerusalem from the mount called Olivet, which is from Jerusalem a sabbath day's journey.*
>
> *And when they were come in, they went up into an upper room, where abode both Peter, and James, and John, and Andrew, Philip, and Thomas, Bartholomew, and Matthew, James the son of Alphaeus, and Simon Zelotes, and Judas the brother of James.*
>
> *These all continued with one accord in prayer and supplication, with the women, and Mary the mother of Jesus, and with His brethren.* (Acts 1:12-14)

k. Show the new believer that he should not neglect to attend church services to worship God on Sunday, the first day of the week. Let him read Hebrews 10:25 with you.

> *Not forsaking the assembling of ourselves together, as the manner of some is; but exhorting one another: and so much the more, as ye see the day approaching.* (Heb. 10:25)

6. Always Worship the Lord With Your Substance

Giving is always a part of a Christian's life in glorifying God. It is acknowledging that everything comes from Him; even a person's own life belongs to God.

If giving is only a gimmick to get rich, then it should be stopped because it is not pleasing in the sight of God.

Tithes and offerings belong to God through the local church, for the support of all its projects, but the first priority is the pastor's support. If you like to give to charitable organizations, that is fine, God is pleased; but your tithes and offerings belong to God through the local church where you are a member.

According to Leland Stowe, someone has said: "Tithing changes people inside, endowing them with new confidence and peace of mind.... Returning a fair share of God's bounty, tithers discovered, not only takes faith but strengthens faith—in life, in others, and in oneself....Tithings keeps the church's activities dignified and concerned with its vital mission" (Stowe, 1958: 3.4).

Those who give their tithes and offerings to God through their local church know that their lives were changed. They have experienced a prosperous life, a happy and wonderful family and home. Their relationships with the church and others were changed. The church became the center of their home; there they have the feeling of belonging, and they love to share the blessings of God with others. The love of Christ is manifested in their lives.

a. Show the new believer that, as a Christian, the offering is a part of the worship service to glorify God. Let him read Psalm 96:8 and Proverbs 3:9 with you.

Give unto the Lord the glory due unto His name: bring an offering, and come into His courts. (Ps. 96:8)

Honour the Lord with thy substance, and with the firstfruits of all thine increase. (Prov. 3:9)

b. Show the new believer that God owns the earth and all that dwells in it, including him. Let him read Psalm 24:1 and First Corinthians 10:26 with you.

The earth is the Lord's, and the fulness thereof; the world, and they that dwell therein. (Ps. 24:1)

For the earth is the Lord's, and the fulness thereof. (I Cor. 10:26)

c. Show the new believer that God gave the most precious gift to him, His only begotten Son. Let him read John 3:16 with you.

For God so loved the world, that He gave His only begotten Son, that whosoever believeth in Him should not perish, but have everlasting life. (John 3:16)

d. Show the new believer that Jesus gave Himself to redeem us. Let him read Titus 2:14 and First Timothy 2:6 with you.

Who gave Himself for us, that He might redeem us from all iniquity, and purify unto Himself a peculiar people, zealous of good works. (Titus 2:14)

Who gave Himself a ransom for all, to be testified in due time. (I Tim. 2:6)

e. Show the new believer that God requires one tenth of his income. Let him read Malachi 3:10 with you.

Bring ye all the tithes into the storehouse, that there may be meat in Mine house, and prove Me now herewith, saith the Lord of hosts, if I will not open you the windows of heaven, and pour you out a blessing, that there shall not be room enough to receive it. (Mal. 3:10)

f. Show the believer that God requires His fair share of His own. Let him read Proverbs 3:9 and 10 with you.

Honour the Lord with thy substance, and with the firstfruits of all thine increase:

So shall thy barns be filled with plenty, and thy presses shall burst out with new wine. (Prov. 3:9,10)

g. Show the believer the more he gives, the more blessings he will receive. Let him read Luke 6:38 with you.

Give, and it shall be given unto you; good measure, pressed down, and shaken together, and running over, shall men give into your bosom... (Luke 6:38)

h. Show the new believer why God requires tithes and offerings. Let him read the following reasons with you:
1) Tithes belong to God.

And all the tithe of the land, whether of the seed of the land, or of the fruit of the tree, is the Lord's, it is holy unto the Lord. (Lev. 27:30)

2) God needs it in His storehouse.

Bring ye all the tithes into the storehouse, that there may be meat in Mine house... (Mal. 3:10)

3) Preachers must live by the gospel.

Even so hath the Lord ordained that they which preach the gospel should live of the gospel. (I Cor. 9:14)

i. Show the new believer who gives, as revealed in the Bible. Let him read, with you, of the following givers:

1) Abel gave the best.

And Abel, he also brought of the firstlings of his flock and of the fat thereof. And the Lord had respect unto Abel and to his offering. (Gen. 4:4)

2) Abraham cheerfully gave his tithe.

And blessed be the most high God, which hath delivered thine enemies into thy hand. And he [Abraham] gave him tithes of all. (Gen. 14:20)

3) The people of God gave their tithes.

Now consider how great this man was, unto whom even the patriarch Abraham gave the tenth of the spoils.

*And verily they that are of the sons of Levi, who receive the office of the priesthood, have a commandment to take **tithes of the people** according to the law, that is, of their brethren, though they come out of the loins of Abraham:*

*But he whose descent is not counted from them received **tithes of Abraham**, and blessed him that had the promises.* (Heb. 7:4-6)

4) The poor widow gave all she had.

*And He called unto Him His disciples, and saith unto them, Verily I say unto you, That this **poor widow** hath cast more in, than all they which have cast into the treasury:*

*For all they did cast in of their abundance; but she of her want did cast in **all that she had**, even **all her living**.* (Mark 12:43,44)

5) Every Christian ought to give their tithes.

Upon the first day of the week let every one of you lay by him in store, as God hath prospered him.... (I Cor. 16:2)

6) Every man (people of God) is to give tithes.

Every man shall give as he is able, according to the blessing of the Lord thy God which He hath given thee. (Deut. 16:17)

j. Show the new believer *how* to give his tithe. Let him read the following with you:
1) Cheerfully put aside for the Lord.

On every Lord's Day each of you should put aside something from what you have earned during the week, and use it for this offering. The amount depends on how much the Lord has helped you earn.... (1 Cor. 16:2 TLB)

2) Cheerfully give.

Every man according as he purposeth in his heart, so let him give; not grudgingly, or of necessity: for God loveth a cheerful giver. (II Cor. 9:7)

k) Show the new believer *when* to give his tithe. Let him read the following with you:
1) On the first day of the week.

Upon the first day of the week let every one of you lay by him in store, as God hath prospered him... (I Cor. 16:2)

l. Show the new believer God's promise of rewards for responding to His demands. They are the following:

1) Your barns to be filled with plenty.

So shall thy barns be filled with plenty, and thy presses shall burst out with new wine. (Prov. 3:10)

2) To receive an overflowing blessing.

...and prove Me now herewith, saith the Lord of hosts, if I will not open you the windows of heaven, and pour you out a blessing, that there shall not be room enough to receive it. (Mal. 3:10)

m. Show the new believer God's warning for not responding to His demands. Let him read the following with you:

1) Beware of covetousness.

And He said unto them, Take heed, and beware of covetousness: for a man's life consisteth not in the abundance of the things which he possesseth. (Luke 12:15)

2) Beware of God's curse.

Will a man rob God? Yet ye have robbed Me. But ye say, Wherein have we robbed Thee? In tithes and offerings.

Ye are cursed with a curse: for ye have robbed Me, even this whole nation. (Mal. 3:8,9)

n. Show the new believer that Jesus Christ commended the poor widow in Mark 12:43 and 44, who gave all that she had. He also commended the practice of tithing, but condemned the impure motives of tithing. Let the new believer read Matthew 23:23 with you.

Woe unto you, scribes and Pharisees, hypocrites! for ye pay tithe of mint and anise and cummin, and have omitted the weightier matters of the law, judgment, mercy, and faith: these ought ye to have done, and not to leave the other undone. (Matt. 23:23)

o. Show the new believer how to calculate his tithe if he is willing and cheerful about giving God His fair share of His own for the glory of His name and for the honor of His Church. So, if the person receives a paycheck of $500 per month, how much will his weekly tithe be?

Solution:

1) Multiply $500 by 10% = $50 as his tithe per month.

2) Multiply $50 by 12 months = $600. This is his tithe for the whole year.

3) Divide $600 by 52 Sundays per year = $11.54. This is his tithe every Sunday, the first day of the week.

If he receives a bonus or other income of $50 within a week, multiply $50 by 10% = $5. Adding $5 to $11.54, his regular tithe = $16.54. This is his tithe for the week he has an extra income.

In this way, the new believer gives his tithe regularly, every first day of the week.

Many Christians do not know how to tithe; others don't care and don't mind. They just give anything, like Cain, who did what he should not have done (Gen. 4:3,7). But look at Abel. He selected the best from the firstborn of his flock and presented them to the Lord. The Lord accepted Abel's offering with favor (Gen. 4:4).

Christians who have experienced the blessings and joy of giving say that giving the tithe is the least they give, and that is biblical. You can give more and give cheerfully. Jesus Christ commended the poor widow who gave only two mites, "all that she had, even all her living" (Mark 12:44). In *The Living Bible* it says: "He called His disciples to Him and remarked, 'That poor widow has given more than all those rich men put together! For they gave a little of their extra fat, while she gave up her last penny' " (Mark 12:43,44). As a Christian, it is the will of God for you to give your tithe. That is the least that you will give, but you can give more cheerfully.

Ready to Be Weaned

The new believer is now ready to be weaned. He is now ready to eat solid food, ready to understand what is good and what is bad in the realm of a Christian life. The Bible says: "But strong meat belongeth to them that are of full age, even those who by reason of use have their senses exercised to discern both good and evil" (Heb. 5:14).

1. Get Him Committed to a Local Church

If the new believer is not yet committed to any local church, and it is impossible for him to join you in your local church, you have not yet reached your goal. Make sure that he becomes a member of a convenient local church that preaches the pure gospel of Jesus Christ, the divine Lord and Savior, and that expectantly waits for His return.

The new believer needs a home church that can take over and continue to nurture and nourish him with spiritual food for his soul. Introduce him to the pastor and make sure that he will be cared for. Jesus said: "Feed My sheep" (John 21:16).

The Last Words of Exhortation

1. *Remind the new believer* of his privileges and opportunities as a child of God, and his responsibilities

and obligations as a member of a local church. Remind him to abide with Jesus Christ as his divine Lord and Savior, and to do His will which is pleasing in His sight.

2. *Instruct him* to continue feeding himself with the precious and nutritious food, the Word of God from above, the Holy Scriptures, by reading his Bible regularly every day, starting from the Gospel of Jesus Christ according to John. It will be easier to understand. Then have him continue reading from the Acts of the Apostles, then to the rest of the books of the New Testament. It would be boring for him to begin reading from Genesis or any other book in the Old Testament.

3. *Encourage him* to attend Bible studies and to share his experiences with the Lord to others. Tell him to give testimonies when opportunities are at hand. Encourage him to attend church services regularly, so he will not become malnourished and anemic, but remain healthy and sound spiritually. The Bible says: "Not forsaking the assembling of ourselves together, as the manner of some is; but exhorting one another: and so much the more, as ye see the day approaching" (Heb. 10:25).

4. *Inspire him* to be faithful to God the Father, who is infinite in wisdom; to Jesus Christ, the only Son, his personal divine Lord and Savior; and to the Holy Spirit, his divine Guide and Comforter. Inspire him to apply what he had learned to his life. Help him to witness for Jesus Christ, so His love can be manifested in his life. The Bible says: "But be ye doers of the word, and not hearers only, deceiving your own selves" (James 1:22). "For thou shalt be His witness unto all men of what thou hast seen and heard" (Acts 22:15).

Appendix A

Dealing With Prospects Who Are Roman Catholics (Romano Catolico)

The soul winner must know the beliefs and doctrines of the *Romano Catolico* and how they differ from those of the Evangelicals or Protestants.

Their Beliefs and Doctrines

The Roman Catholic Church still believes and teaches the following practices and traditions: baptismal regeneration; justification by works; image worship; celebacy; indulgence; Mariolatry; confessional; purgatory; transubstantiation; and penance. These heathen beliefs and traditions were introduced during the reign of Boniface III in A.D. 606 (Larkin 1920:[50]).

By observance of those traditions, Catholics hope to gain entrance to Heaven. Salvation, for them, is uncertain. They do not know whether or not they are saved. They don't have the assurance of salvation. To them, salvation is a future hope.

They also believe that salvation is obtained through the intermediary of the Church, the priests, the Saints and the Virgin Mary.

The Roman Catholic Church believes and teaches that the Bible is not sufficient and does not contain all the truth as a rule of faith and practice. This is how Dr. Sanders described the Roman Catholic beliefs and doctrines in *Our Protestant Faith*:

The Catholic is taught that the Scriptures are not sufficient as a rule of faith and practice. The Roman Church believes that the Bible does not contain all necessary revealed truths. Thus, it has placed side by side with the Scriptures a *supposed* body of the teachings of Christ and the apostles which is *claimed* were handed down *by word of mouth* and finally put in written form. The Roman Catholic has made these traditional sayings of equal value with the Scriptures themselves. Moreover, the teaching of Rome is that only the Church has the competency and the right to interpret this two-fold body (Scripture and tradition), and its interpretation must be regarded as infallible. Accordingly, through the centuries Catholic[s] have been discouraged from seeking God and truth through their own reading or study of the Bible (nd:5).

Dr. Sanders further states that the Roman Catholic has given greater authority to the tradition rather than to the teachings of the Bible, even though the traditions contradict the teachings of the Bible. "Tradition is therefore used to interpret the Bible instead of the Bible interpreting the tradition, which is the Protestant position" (nd:6).

An example of this tradition is their belief that "the Virgin Mary is a Co-Redeemer with her son." Another tradition is that the Roman Church and the Pope are "infallible." They cannot be wrong on matters of "faith and morals" (nd:6).

Regarding salvation, Dr. Sanders recorded several doctrines on which the Roman Church based their salvation.

1. The Roman Church believes and teaches that salvation can be achieved "through 'mental faith.'" The Athanasian Creed says:

"Whoever would be saved, must first of all take care that he hold the Catholic faith. Which, if except a man preserve whole and inviolate, he shall without doubt perish eternally." The decrees of the council of Trent declare, "The Church of Rome is the mother and the mistress of all churches, and to believe her so to be, is necessary to salvation" (nd:19).

2. The Roman Church believes and teaches that salvation can be achieved through "the sacraments

[which are] are necessary for salvation." The people were "taught that there is no salvation apart from baptism" (nd:20).

3. The "Roman Catholics claim that salvation comes through the intercession of the Virgin Mary and the Saints" (nd:20).

4. The "Romanist doctrine teaches the necessity of the sufferings of Purgatory for salvation." The Roman Church believes and teaches that suffering in purgatory is necessary for salvation. The Church has the power to shorten the process of suffering in purgatory by having a priest say a mass on behalf of the dead. However, that can be done only if the relative of the dead person will pay a certain amount of money to the officiating priest (nd:21).

In short, the Roman Catholic Church's doctrine about salvation says that the benefits of Jesus Christ's redemptive work can come only through faith in the Church's doctrines, "by submission to her sacraments, by performing good works, by the intercession of Mary and by an indefinite residence in purgatory" (nd:22).

How to Deal With the Romano Catolico

The soul winner must not argue with the prospect about his religious beliefs. Instead, he must talk about the similarities of the Catholic beliefs with that of the Evangelicals. Do not ask the prospect if he is a Christian because Catholics believe that when one is baptized, he becomes a Christian. Do not even ask him if he is a born again Christian because some have claimed to be born again after attending the "Consortium" a sort of spiritual retreat. What the soul winner should ask him is: "Where will you go when you die, or when you leave this world?" The answer for sure is, "Nobody knows," or a few might say, "To heaven, I hope." Now ask the prospect if he wants to know for sure where will he go when he dies, or when he leaves this world.

1. Show the prospect that it is the will of God that we know that we are saved or have eternal life. Let him read First John 5:13 with you. (Use a Roman Catholic Bible, if possible.)

These things have I written unto you that believe on the name of the Son of God; that ye may know that ye have eternal life, and that ye may believe on the name of the Son of God. (John 5:13)

2. Show the prospect that all are sinners before God; including you first and the prospect last. Let him read Romans 3:10 and 23 with you.

As it is written, There is none righteous, no, not one.

For all have sinned, and come short of the glory of God. (Rom. 3:10,23)

3. Show the prospect that even the apostle Paul admitted that he himself was a sinner. Let him read Romans 5:8 with you.

But God commendeth His love toward us, in that, while we were yet sinners, Christ died for us. (Rom. 5:8)

Now ask the person if he admits that he is a sinner according to the Bible.

4. Show the prospect that the wages of sin is death. Let him read Romans 6:23 with you.

For the wages of sin is death; but the gift of God is eternal life through Jesus Christ our Lord. (Rom. 6:23)

5. Show the prospect that, since all are sinners, all will suffer eternally in the lake of fire. Let him read Revelation 20:14 and 21:8 with you.

And death and hell were cast into the lake of fire. This is the second death. (Rev. 20:14)

But the fearful, and unbelieving, and the abominable, and murderers, and whoremongers, and sorcerers, and idolaters, and all liars, shall have their part in the lake which burneth with fire and brimstone: which is the second death. (Rev. 21:8)

Now ask him if he wants to suffer eternally in the lake of fire. Of course the answer is no. Nobody wants to suffer in the lake of fire eternally. Show him the way to salvation.

Lead Him to Faith in Jesus Christ as His Personal Lord and Savior

At this point, the prospect might be scared and ask you how he can be saved. That is the right time to guide him to Jesus. Don't let that opportunity slip away.

1. Show the prospect that God has a plan of salvation for all His creation. Let him read John 3:16 with you.

For God so loved the world, that He gave His only begotten Son, that whosoever believeth in Him should not perish, but have everlasting life. (John 3:16)

2. Show the prospect that the only way to escape punishment and torture in the lake of fire is to believe

in Jesus Christ. Those who don't believe are already condemned. Let him read John 3:18 and 36 with you.

He that believeth on Him is not condemned: but he that believeth not is condemned already, because he hath not believed in the name of the only begotten Son of God.

He that believeth on the Son hath everlasting life: and he that believeth not the Son shall not see life; but the wrath of God abideth on him. (John 3:18,36)

Continue leading the prospect to faith in Jesus Christ as his personal Lord and Savior by using the steps of salvation in Section A of Chapter IX in this book.

If he is not yet convinced, he still has a second chance before he dies. But after death, there is no second chance.

Now Is the Day of Salvation

1. Show the prospect that there is no reference in the Bible to prove that salvation is obtained through the intermediary of the Church, the priests, the Saints and the Virgin Mary. Only Jesus Christ is the mediator between God and man. Let him read First Timothy 2:5 with you.

For there is one God, and one mediator between God and men, the man Christ Jesus. (I Tim. 2:5)

2. Show the prospect that the Bible teaches us to worship God and God only; not the saints, not the Virgin Mary, not the pope or the priests, for they are human beings like us. Let him read Acts 10:25 and 26 with you.

And as Peter was coming in, Cornelius met him, and fell down at his feet, and worshipped him.

But Peter took him up, saying, Stand up; I myself also am a man. (Acts 10:25,26)

3. Show the prospect that he is already condemned. When he dies, there will be no second chance. But if he believes and receives Jesus Christ now as his personal Lord and Savior, before he dies, there is still a second chance. Let him read John 3:18 with you.

He that believeth on Him is not condemned: but he that believeth not is condemned already, because he hath not believed in the name of the only begotten Son of God. (John 3:18)

4. Show the prospect that he is bound for hell and the lake of fire to be tortured eternally if he refuses to believe now. "...now is the accepted time; behold, now is the day of salvation." Tomorrow might be too late. What if he dies tonight? There will be no more chances. Let him read Second Corinthians 6:2 with you.

(For He saith, I have heard thee in a time accepted, and in the day of salvation have I succoured thee: behold, now is the accepted time; behold, now is the day of salvation.) (II Cor. 6:2)

5. Show the prospect that the sacrament of baptism has nothing to do with salvation; neither can he buy it or work for it. Let him read Ephesians 2:8 and 9 with you:

For by grace are ye saved through faith; and that not of yourselves: it is the gift of God:

Not of works, lest any man should boast. (Eph. 2:8,9)

6. Show the prospect that the doctrine of purgatory is not taught in the Bible. Tell him that the Bible speaks only of Heaven and hell, not a waiting place for souls after death. Let him know that those who are in hell cannot be transferred to Heaven. Read Luke 16:19-26.

There was a certain rich man, which was clothed in purple and fine linen, and fared sumptuously every day:

And there was a certain beggar named Lazarus, which was laid at his gate, full of sores,

And desiring to be fed with the crumbs which fell from the rich man's table: moreover the dogs came and licked his sores.

And it came to pass, that the beggar died, and was carried by the angels into Abraham's bosom [heaven]: the rich man also died, and was buried;

And in hell he lift up his eyes, being in torments, and seeth Abraham afar off, and Lazarus in his bosom.

And he cried and said, Father Abraham, have mercy on me, and send Lazarus, that he may dip the tip of his finger in water, and cool my tongue; for I am tormented in this flame.

But Abraham said, Son, remember that thou in thy lifetime receivedst thy good things, and likewise Lazarus evil things: but now he is comforted, and thou art tormented.

And beside all this, between us and you there is a great gulf fixed: so that they which would pass from hence to you cannot; neither can they pass to us, that would come from thence. (Luke 16:19-26)

7. Show the prospect that he needs to be born again, or born of the Spirit, to enter the Kingdom of God. Let him read John 3:3 and 5 with you.

Jesus answered and said unto him, Verily, verily, I say unto thee, Except a man be born again, he cannot see the kingdom of God.

Jesus answered, Verily, verily, I say unto thee, Except a man be born of water [the flesh] *and of the Spirit, he cannot enter into the kingdom of God.* (John 3:3,5)

8. Show the prospect that, if he believes and accepts Jesus Christ as his personal divine Lord and Savior now before he dies, he will go to Heaven. Let him read Luke 23:43 with you.

And Jesus said unto him, Verily I say unto thee, Today shalt thou be with Me in paradise. (Luke 23:43)

At this point the prospect is interested in knowing the way of salvation and asks you what he needs to do to be saved. Show him the plan of salvation by using Section A of Chapter IX in this book. If he claims to be religious, use Section D. If he claims to be righteous, use Section C. If he is not interested in the salvation of his soul, then use Section B.

Appendix B

Dealing With Prospects Who Are of The Philippine Independent Church

This church was established simultaneously with the revolution movement in the Philippines, with the concept of forming a national church that was independent from Rome. As a result, the church was proclaimed in Manila on October 17, 1902; and in January 3, 1903, Gregorio Aglipay was consecrated as the Supreme Bishop of the new church.

Since celibacy is the only major difference between their beliefs and the doctrines of the Roman Catholic Church, we apply the same approach and methods we use with members of the Roman Catholic Church.

Appendix C

Dealing With Prospects Who Are of the Church of Jesus Christ of the Latter Day Saints

The Church of Jesus Christ of the Latter Day Saints, commonly known as the Mormon Church, organized in 1829, is one of the cults listed in The Kingdom of the Cults by Dr. Walter Martin.

Their Background

Joseph Smith, Jr. is the founder of the Mormon Church. He started out in Fayette, New York, but later moved to Kirtland, Ohio, because the people who knew him in New York regarded him as having a bad reputation and being untrustworthy.

According to Mr. Kenneth Boa, Joseph Smith claimed to have received a vision in 1820 in which God the Father and the Son appeared to him. "[H]e was told in this vision that all the churches were abominations to God and that he was being charged as a prophet to restore the true gospel to the world" (1980:65).

Smith claimed that the angel Moroni appeared to him and told him about the golden plates, which he later interpreted. His interpretation became known as "The Book of Mormon." The Mormons consider it and all his "writings on a higher plane than the Bible. It says that the Bible is at variance with Mormon doctrine, [that] the Bible is incorrectly translated" (Boa 1980:71,72).

In 1839 Joseph Smith, Jr. and his followers were required to leave Ohio and Missouri. They were accused of "a number of crimes...by the order of Governor Boggs..." (Boa 1980:65). So Joseph Smith, Jr. led his followers to Illinois, where he introduced the practice of polygamy to his followers. Smith and his brother Hyrum were jailed because they "tried to destroy a local newspaper office" for exposing their immoralities. While they waited for their trial, an "angry mob stormed the jail on June 27, 1844 and shot Smith and his brother, thus making them martyrs for the cause of mormonism" (Boa 1980:66).

Brigham Young succeeded Joseph Smith, Jr. as leader. He too was a prophet of the Mormon Church.

Dealing With Prospects of the Latter Day Saints Church

He led the Mormons to Salt Lake, Utah, in July 1847. He too "encourage[d] the practice of polygamy and took 25 wives for himself" (Boa 1980:66). Polygamy is a very important teaching of the Mormon Church. Since the government is against this immoral practice, the Mormons substituted this practice with the "celestial marriage." "Since the Mormons were forced to abandon this practice [polygamy] in 1890, they have substituted the practice of 'celestial marriage.' Marriages must be sealed in the Mormon secret temples in order for them to endure for eternity. A man can seal up for himself several wives for the future life by engaging in special rites in Mormon temples" (Boa 1980:71).

Brigham Young's desperate desire to control Utah led to the massacre which he ordered of more than 100 new, non-Mormon immigrants. This is how Dr. Martin describes the situation:

> One such evidence of his determination to control Utah was the order which he gave to massacre over 100 non-Mormon immigrants in what has now become known as the infamous Mountain Meadows massacre. In this particular instance, for reasons known only to himself, Young entrusted to Bishop John D. Lee in 1857 the task of annihilating a wagon train of virtually helpless immigrants. This, Bishop Lee did faithfully, and 20 years later he was imprisoned, tried, convicted and executed by the Government of the United States for this vicious, totalitarian action (1980: 176).

Mr. Kenneth Boa described the incident as "One of the lowest points in Mormon history..." (1980:66). He also described the Mormon Church as "the most effective counterfeits of biblical Christianity ever devised" (1980:64).

The Book of Mormon is an expansion of the "Manuscript Found," whose author was a retired minister. Mr. Boa wrote:

> Most researchers on the subject agree that The Book of Mormon is actually Smith's expansion of Romance called Manuscript Found, written by a retired minister named Solomon Spaulding. The story behind Smith's "translation" of the Pearl of Great Price is even more bizarre. Smith purportedly bought from a traveling showman some mummies which were wrapped in papyrus sheets containing the writings of Abraham! (1980:69)

According to Robert and Gretchen Passantino, The Book of Mormon did not come from the "God of the Bible." They wrote:

> Although the true origin of The Book of Mormon may never be known positively, we can confidently state that its origin is not with the God of the Bible. Not only does The Book of Mormon contradict the Bible in numerous places, but it is full of archeological errors. Today's version has more than 3900 changes from [the] 1830 edition of "the most correct of any book on earth," which was probably an adulterated form of a historical novel written before 1816 by Rev. Samuel Spalding (1981:96,97) (Must be Solomon Spaulding.)

The Passantinos further state that "...we need to remind ourselves of the fact that the cults, including Mormonism, take the vocabulary of the Bible and redefine it to fit their own views" (1981:93).

The Book of Mormon, according to Mr. Kenneth Boa, was copied from the Bible. Mr. Boa wrote:

Though The Book of Mormon was buried in A.D. 428, it contains about 25,000 words verbatim from [the] A.D. 1611 King James version of the Bible! This is a 1,200 to 2,200 year anachronism (depending on what book within The Book of Mormon is being considered). The words of Christ, Peter, Paul, John, and other New Testament writers are indiscriminately placed in the mouths of people who lived centuries before Christ, and all copied from the King James version...In addition to these obvious plagiarisms, The Book of Mormon is written in a wordy imitation of the biblical style of the early 17th century (1980:68).

As an example, the Book of Isaiah, chapters 2 through 14, were copied word for word by Smith in The Book of Mormon, 2 Nephi, chapters 12 through 24. Smith only changed the name of the book and the numbers of the chapters. Another example is 3 Nephi, chapters 12 through 14, which were copied from Matthew chapters 5 through 7.

Their Beliefs and Doctrines

The soul winner must be familiar with the beliefs and doctrines of the Mormons. They believe in Joseph

Smith, Jr., who claimed to be the prophet. They believe and teach that there are many gods, once human beings, who have bodies: flesh and bones. Each member of the Mormon Church is taught how to become a god himself. Dr. Martin quoted from the Mormon Journal, which says:

> "Gods exist, and had better strive to be prepared to be one of them" (Brigham Young, *Journal of Discourses*, Vol. 7, p. 238 as quoted in Martin 1985:202,203).

In corroboration with those statements, Robert and Gretchen Passantino state:

> Polytheism is the belief in more than one true God, even if no more than one god is worshipped. Joseph Smith asserted the existence of more than one God in the history of the Church (6:305-306): "You have got to learn how to be gods yourselves, and to be kings and priests to God, the same as all gods have done before you...." We could properly say that the Mormons are henotheistic, a form of polytheism which means that you worship one god out of the many gods in existence (1981:100).

The Mormons believe and teach that the birth of Jesus Christ was the result of the sexual relations between God the Father and Mary, as quoted by Dr. Martin in his *Cults Reference Bible*: "The Father had sexual relations with Mary to produce Jesus' body" (1981:795). If that is true, then Mary would have not been a virgin before she gave birth to Jesus.

Salvation, to the Mormons, is by faith in Jesus Christ and by obedience of the laws and ordinances. This is how Dr. Martin describes their beliefs regarding salvation:

> The Mormon doctrine of salvation involves not only faith in Christ, but baptism of immersion, obedience to the teaching of the Mormon Church, good works, and "keeping the commandments of God (which) will cleanse away the stain of sin" (*Journal of Discourses,* Vol. 2, p. 4 as quoted in Martin (1985:216).

The Mormons believe and teach that "all men are saved by grace alone without any act on their part" (see the following quote). This sounds rather Evangelical, but they interpret it to fit their doctrine. This is their interpretation, as quoted by Dr. Martin:

> Grace is simply the mercy, the love and the condescension God has for his children, as a result of which he has ordained the plan of salvation so that they may have power to progress and became like him...All men are saved by grace alone without any act on their part, meaning that they are resurrected and become immortal because of the atoning sacrifice of Christ...In addition to this redemption from death, all men, by the grace of God, have power to gain eternal life. This is called salvation by grace coupled with obedience to the laws and ordinances of the gospel (1985:220,221).

How to Deal With the Mormon

When you come across a Mormon prospect, don't allow him to control the conversation. Before he starts reciting a list of Bible verses, ask him if he would like to study the Scriptures with you and see what the Bible actually says. Begin with the God of the Bible.

About God the Father

1. Show the prospect that the Bible teaches only one God for the Christians. Let him read First Corinthians 8:5 and 6 with you.

For though there be that are called gods, whether in heaven or in earth, (as there be gods many, and lords many,)

But to us there is but one God, the Father, of whom are all things, and we in Him; and one Lord Jesus Christ, by whom are all things, and we by Him. (I Cor. 8:5,6)

2. Show the prospect that there is no other God beside Him. Read Isaiah 43:10 and 11 and 45:5 and 22.

Ye are My witnesses, saith the Lord, and My servant whom I have chosen; that ye may know and believe Me, and understand that I am He; before Me there was no God formed, neither shall there be after Me.

I, even I, am the Lord; and beside Me there is no saviour. (Isa. 43:10,11)

I am the Lord, and there is none else, there is no God beside Me...

Look unto Me, and be ye saved, all the ends of the earth: for I am God, and there is none else. (Isa. 45:5,22)

3. Show the prospect that the God in Genesis 1:1 refers to the three persons in the Godhead. God, in Hebrew, according to Dr. Berkhof, is *Elohim,* the plural of *Eloah* (1985:48).

Corroborating those statements, Dr. Billy Graham said that, according to a Hebrew scholar, there are three numbers in the Hebrew language. They are: "Singular, one; dual, two; plural, more than two" (1978:29). Now let the prospect read Genesis 1:1 and 26; 3:22; 11:6 and 7 and Isaiah 6:8 with you.

In the beginning God created the heaven and the earth.

And God said, Let Us make man in Our image, after Our likeness... (Gen. 1:1,26)

And the Lord God said, Behold, the man is become as one of Us... (Gen. 3:22)

And the Lord said...

Go to, let Us go down, and there confound their language... (Gen. 11:6,7)

Also I heard the voice of the Lord, saying, Whom shall I send, and who will go for Us... (Isa. 6:8)

About Jesus Christ the Son

If there was a sexual relation between God and Mary, as claimed by the Mormons, Mary would have not been a virgin when she gave birth to Jesus.

1. Show the prospect that Mary was a virgin when she gave birth to Jesus Christ. Let him read Matthew 1:23 with you.

Behold, a virgin shall be with child, and shall bring forth a son, and they shall call His name Emmanuel, which being interpreted is, God with us. (Matt. 1:23)

Verse 25 from The Living Bible says:

"but she remained a virgin until her Son was born; and Joseph named Him 'Jesus.' " (Matt. 1:25 TLB)

2. Show the prospect that Jesus Christ is self-existent, and the Creator of everything that exists. Let him read John 1:1-3 with you.

Before anything else existed, there was Christ, with God. He has always been alive and is Himself God.

He created everything there is—nothing exists that He didn't make. (John 1:1-3 TLB)

3. Show the prospect that God the Son became a man for a mission. Let him read John 1:14 from The Living Bible with you.

And Christ became a human being and lived here on earth amont us and was full of loving forgiveness and truth. And some of us have seen His glory—the glory of the only Son of the heavenly Father! (John 1:14 TLB)

About Salvation

Salvation of the soul is the goal of most people. They do everything in their power to save their souls.

1. Show the prospect that not all who pray and worship God will go to Heaven. Let him read Matthew 7:21 with you.

Not every one that saith unto Me, Lord, Lord, shall enter into the kingdom of heaven; but he that doeth the will of My Father which is in heaven. (Matt. 7:21)

2. Show the prospect that he cannot buy or work for his salvation. Let him read Ephesians 2:8 and 9 with you.

For by grace are ye saved through faith; and that not of yourselves: it is the gift of God:

Not of works, lest any man should boast. (Eph. 2:8,9)

3. The prospect might refer you to Philippians 2:12c, which says: "work out your own salvation with fear and trembling." Show the prospect that this phrase means to do the right thing as a result of being saved. Let him read verses 12 and 13 from The Living Bible with you.

Dearest friends, when I was there with you, you were always so careful to follow my instructions. And now that I am away you must be even more careful to do the good things that result from being saved, obeying God with deep reverence, shrinking back from all that might displease Him.

For God is at work within you, helping you want to obey Him, and then helping you do what He wants. (Phil. 2:12,13 TLB)

4. Show the prospect that baptism has nothing to do with salvation. He might refer you to Mark 16:16a, which says: "He that believeth and is baptized shall be

saved" but the second phrase states that only those who refuse to believe are condemned. Furthermore, we cannot find any verse to corroborate the idea that baptism concerns salvation. Let him read the whole verse with you.

He that believeth and is baptized shall be saved; but he that believeth not shall be damned. (Mark 16:16)

Lead Him to Faith in Jesus Christ

Lead the prospect to believe and accept Jesus Christ as his personal Lord and Savior, that he too may experience the joy of His salvation. Show him God's plan of salvation by using this book's Chapter IX, Section A, if he is interested. If he claims to be religious, use Section D. If he claims to be righteous, use Section C. If he is not interested in the salvation of his soul, use Section B of chapter IX of this book.

Appendix D

Dealing With Prospects Who Are of the Seventh Day Adventist Church

The Seventh Day Adventist Church, commonly known as SDA or Sabatista, is also one of the organizations that continue to grow in numbers and strength. The Evangelical scholars of the Bible were divided when classifying the SDA, whether or not they are a non-Christian cult. Those who classify the SDA as a non-Christian cult, as stated by Dr. Walter Martin, were Louis T. Talbot, M.R. DeHaan, John R. Rice, Anthony A. Hoekema, J.K. Van Baalen, Herbert Bird and John R. Gerstner. Donald Grey Barnhouse, E. Schuyler

English and Walter Martin were convinced that the SDA is not a cult, although they are "definitely out of the mainstream of historic Christian theology..." (Martin 1985:409). This evaluation by Dr. Martin was the result of his interview with the present leaders of the SDA, who sounded like evangelicals.

Mr. Kenneth Boa also made this observation about the beliefs and teachings of the SDA:

> Evangelical scholars differ over the question of whether Seventh Day Adventism should be classed as a cult or as a Christian denomination. Adventism has undergone significant changes over the decades, and today appears to hold an orthodox view of the cardinal Christian doctrines. Thus, it would seem improper to classify Adventism in the same category with such as Mormonism, Christian Science, and Jehovah's Witnesses. Nevertheless, definite doctrinal problems and emphases remain which make it hard to view the Seventh-Day Adventists as just another branch of evangelical Christianity (1980:90).

Their Background, Beliefs and Doctrines

William Miller is one of the influential people in the formation of the SDA. Miller was a Baptist minister who prophesied the advent of Jesus Christ. He predicted that Jesus Christ would come "between March 21, 1843 and March 21, 1844.... But March 21, 1844 came and went without Christ's return" (Boa 1980:90). Miller acknowledged that he made a mistake in his prediction, and because of this mistake, he stopped predicting. According to Mr. Boa, Mr. Miller "never accepted the Seventh Day

Adventist's doctrine and he remained a devout Christian until his death" (1980:91).

According to Mr. Boa, Samuel Show, a follower of William Miller, gave another prediction. He said that the real date of Jesus' coming was October 22, 1844. But although October 22, 1844, came, Jesus Christ did not.

Another follower of Miller was Hiram Edson. He also gave a false prediction. He defended Miller by saying that Jesus Christ actually came, just in another place.

Joseph Bates was another follower of Miller "who taught that Saturday Sabbath was a perpetual ordinance which the Church should practice today" (Boa 1980:91).

The third follower of Miller and the foremost leader of the SDA was Ellen G. White. The members of the SDA believed her to be a prophet. The "Seventh-Day Adventists insist that the 'Spirit of prophecy' was exclusively given to her. They claim that her interpretations of the Bible are inspired." Some even believed that her "writings [were] on a par with the Scripture..." (Boa 1980:91,92).

Boa's evaluation of the writings of Ellen White is, the members of the SDA believed them to be "divinely authoritative." Boa wrote:

Seventh-Day Adventists have revered Ellen G. White and her writings to a dangerous extent. In practice, her interpretations are accepted as divinely authoritative. Adventists have distorted several spiritual teachings in order to support Mrs. White's "visions" (1980:96).

According to Dr. Walter Martin, the SDA divided doctrinally into two groups. One group consists of those leaders and members whose beliefs are within the evangelical teachings, while the other group are leaders and members who support Ellen G. White in her prophetic views and observance of the laws. This is how Dr. Martin described the situation:

> Doctrinally, the church has developed a large rift between those members and leaders who are solidly within the evangelical Christian camp and those members and leaders who, because of their emphasis on works-righteousness, legalism, and the prophetic status accorded the founder Ellen G. White, may well move the denomination over time outside of the evangelical camp and perhaps even into actual cultism (1985:410).

How to Deal With the Seventh Day Adventist

The soul winner must be familiar with the beliefs and doctrines of the SDA. The fundamental belief and doctrine of the SDA is the absolute necessity of worshiping on the seventh day of the week, which is Saturday. They believe and teach that those who worship the Lord on Sundays instead of Saturdays will have the mark of the beast upon them and that they, therefore, cannot be saved (Boa 1980:93).

You must know their favorite verses and how they interpret them out of context. Whenever they come across the word *commandment,* they mean the Ten Commandments or the Sabbath. Take First John 2:4 and First John 3:23, for example.

> *He that saith, I know Him, and keepeth not His commandments, is a liar, and the truth is not in Him.* (I John 2:4)

Compare this verse with the one from The Living Bible and notice that *commandment* doesn't mean the Ten Commandments or the Sabbath as they claim.

Someone may say, "I am a Christian; I am on my way to heaven; I belong to Christ." But if he doesn't do what Christ tells him to, he is a liar. (1 John 2:4 TLB)

And this is His commandment, That we should believe on the name of His Son Jesus Christ, and love one another, as He gave us commandment. (I John 3:23)

Again, compare this verse with the one from The Living Bible and see that the Adventists' interpretation is lifted out of context.

And this is what God says we must do: Believe on the name of His Son Jesus Christ, and love one another. (1 John 3:23)

There are many other verses where *commandment* doesn't mean the Ten Commandments. So, when you come across an SDA prospect, invite him to study the Bible with you and to discover the context, what the Scriptures really mean. Begin with the laws.

The Observance of the Law

1. Show the prospect that Christians are no longer under the law. Let him read Galatians 3:23-25 and 5:18 with you.

But before faith came, we were kept under the law, shut up unto the faith which should afterwards be revealed.

Wherefore the law was our schoolmaster to bring us unto Christ, that we might be justified by faith.

But after that faith is come, we are no longer under a schoolmaster. (Gal. 3:23-25)

But if ye be led of the Spirit, ye are not under the law. (Gal. 5:18)

2. Show the prospect that all believers are under the law of Jesus Christ. Let him read Romans 7:4 with you.

Wherefore, my brethren, ye also are become dead to the law by the body of Christ; that ye should be married to another, even to Him who is raised from the dead, that we should bring forth fruit unto God. (Rom. 7:4)

3. Show the prospect that the law of commandments was abolished by Jesus Christ. Let him read Ephesians 2:15 with you.

Having abolished in His flesh the enmity, even the law of commandments contained in ordinances; for to make in Himself of twain one new man, so making peace. (Eph. 2:15)

4. Show the prospect that the law was terminated in Jesus Christ. Let him read Romans 10:4 with you.

For Christ is the end of the law for righteousness to every one that believeth. (Rom. 10:4)

The Observance of the Sabbath

1. Show the prospect that the Sabbath was a sign between God and Israel. Let him read Exodus 31:12 and 13 with you.

And the Lord spake unto Moses, saying,

Speak thou also unto the children of Israel, saying, Verily My sabbaths ye shall keep: for it is a sign between Me and you throughout your generations; that ye may know that I am the Lord that doth sanctify you (Ex. 31:12,13).

2. Show the prospect that Jesus Christ and His disciples did not observe the Sabbath day. Let him read Matthew 12:1 and 2 with you.

At that time Jesus went on the sabbath day through the corn; and His disciples were an hungered, and began to pluck the ears of corn, and to eat.

But when the Pharisees saw it, they said unto Him, Behold, Thy disciples do that which is not lawful to do upon the sabbath day. (Matt. 12:1,2)

The Lord's Day

1. Show the prospect that Jesus Christ was resurrected from the dead on the first day of the week, which is Sunday, and summoned His disciples to assemble in Galilee to meet Him there. Let him read Matthew 28:8-10 with you.

And they departed quickly from the sepulchre with fear and great joy; and did run to bring His disciples word.

And as they went to tell His disciples, behold, Jesus met them, saying, All hail. And they came and held Him by the feet, and worshipped Him.

Then said Jesus unto them, Be not afraid: go tell My brethren that they go into Galilee, and there shall they see Me. (Matt. 28:8-10)

2. Show the prospect that Jesus appeared to His disciples in Galilee and they worshiped Him that Sunday. Let him read Matthew 28:16 and 17 with you.

Then the eleven disciples went away into Galilee, into a mountain where Jesus had appointed them.

And when they saw Him, they worshipped Him: but some doubted. (Matt. 28:16,17)

3. Show the prospect that the disciples assembled again on the following Sunday to worship Jesus who also appeared to them then. Let him read John 20:26 with you.

And after eight days [that is, Sunday] *again His disciples were within, and Thomas with them: then came Jesus, the doors being shut, and stood in the midst, and said, Peace be unto you.* (John 20:26)

4. Show the prospect that the disciples continued to assemble on Sunday, the first day of the week, to worship the Lord and to preach His gospel. Let him read Acts 20:7 with you.

And upon the first day of the week, when the disciples came together to break bread, Paul preached unto them, ready to depart on the morrow; and continued his speech until midnight. (Acts 20:7)

5. Show the prospect that giving is a part of worship on the first day of the week. Let him read First Corinthians 16:1 and 2 with you.

Now concerning the collection for the saints, as I have given order to the churches of Galatia, even so do ye.

Upon the first day of the week let every one of you lay by him in store, as God hath prospered him, that there be no gatherings when I come. (I Cor. 16:1,2)

6. Show the prospect that Sunday, the first day of the week, is the Lord's Day. Let him read Revelation 1:9 and 10 with you.

I John, who also am your brother, and companion in tribulation, and in the kingdom and patience of Jesus Christ, was in the isle that is called Patmos, for the word of God, and for the testimony of Jesus Christ.

I was in the Spirit on the Lord's day, and heard behind me a great voice, as of a trumpet. (Rev. 1:9,10)

7. Show the prospect that in its beginning the church gathered on Sunday, in an upper room. Let him read Acts 1:12-14 with you.

Then returned they unto Jerusalem from the mount called Olivet, which is from Jerusalem a sabbath day's journey.

And when they were come in, they went up into an upper room, where abode both Peter, and James, and John, and Andrew, Philip, and Thomas, Bartholomew, and Matthew, James the son of Alphaeus, and Simon Zelotes, and Judas the brother of James.

These all continued with one accord in prayer and supplication, with the women, and Mary the mother of Jesus, and with His brethren. (Acts 1:12-14)

Abstaining From Certain Food

The soul winner must remember that he is dealing with two groups of the SDA. According to Dr. Martin, one group claims that they refrain from eating certain foods based on health. It is just a careful selection of diet. It is not because of the law and it is not a religious prohibition (1985:431). The other group does not eat anything that is prohibited in the Old Testament. These are the ones who stand behind the teachings of Ellen White.

1. Show the prospect that it will not make him better or worse if he does or does not eat the things that are prohibited in the Old Testament. Let him read First Corinthians 8:8 with you.

> *But meat commendeth us not to God: for neither, if we eat, are we the better; neither, if we eat not, are we the worse.* (I Cor. 8:8)

2. Show the prospect that he will not be condemned by what he eats or drinks or by what days, holy days or Sabbath days he celebrates. Let him read Colossians 2:16 with you.

> *Let no man therefore judge you in meat, or in drink, or in respect of an holyday, or of the new moon, or of the sabbath days.* (Col. 2:16)

Their Beliefs About Salvation

Again, the soul winner must remember that there are two groups in the SDA. The group that Dr. Walter Martin interviewed says that salvation is only by the saving grace of God. There is no salvation through the law or human works of the law. This is their belief about salvation, as quoted by Dr. Martin:

> Salvation is not now, and never has been, by law or by works; salvation is only by the grace of Christ. Moreover, there never was a time in the plan of God when salvation was by human works

or effort. Nothing men can do, or have done, can in any way merit salvation (1985:494).

This group sounds like evangelicals. There are no arguments in this regard. But, in practice, they emphasize the Sabbath keeping and the obedience to the Ten Commandments. Mr. Kenneth Boa described the position of the SDA. He wrote:

> Theory differs from practice, however, and in practical sense, Mrs. White's interpretations of the Bible are accepted without reservation by Adventists as completely authoritative. Apart from her "revelations" and writings it is doubtful that the Seventh-Day Adventist Church would exist today. Whatever follows the standard Adventist phrase "Ellen G. White comments" is regarded as the last word in interpretation regardless of how many biblical scholars disagree (1980:93).

Mr. Kenneth Boa must have been describing the other group, the ones who stood behind Mrs. Ellen White. To lure their prospects, they always refer to James 2:10, which is, if you keep the nine commandments and break just one, you are guilty of them all. So they must keep the Ten Commandments; particularly the seventh day keeping.

James 2:10 actually means that one sin, however insignificant it is, will gradually cause the sinner to be guilty of the whole law of God, the Ten Commandments, which will put him under God's condemnation. So the context is, get away from sin no matter how great or small. We must avoid wallowing in sin.

1. Show the prospect that a person who keeps each of the Ten Commandments is still lost. Let him read Luke 18:20-23 with you.

Thou knowest the commandments, Do not commit adultery, Do not kill, Do not steal, Do not bear false witness, Honour thy father and thy mother.

And he said, All these have I kept from my youth up.

Now when Jesus heard these things, He said unto him, Yet lackest thou one thing: sell all that thou hast, and distribute unto the poor, and thous shalt have treasure in heaven: and come, follow Me.

And when he heard this, he was very sorrowful: for he was very rich. (Luke 18:20-23)

2. Show the prospect that salvation is a gift from God. He cannot work for it; neither can he buy it. Let him read Ephesians 2:8 and 9 with you.

For by grace are ye saved through faith; and that not of yourselves: it is the gift of God:

Not of works, lest any man should boast. (Eph. 2:8,9)

3. Show the prospect that obedience to the law, the Ten Commandments has nothing to do with salvation. Let him read Romans 3:20 with you.

Therefore by the deeds of the law there shall no flesh be justified in His sight: for by the law is the knowledge of sin. (Rom. 3:20)

4. Show the prospect that all have sinned, including yourself. Let him read Romans 3:10 and 23 with you.

Dealing With Prospects of Seventh Day Adventist Church

As it is written, There is none righteous, no, not one.

For all have sinned, and come short of the glory of God. (Rom. 3:10,23)

5. Show the prospect that, according to the Bible, he is a sinner before God. He might say that he did not commit any sin, but let him read First John 1:8 and 10 with you.

If we say that we have no sin, we deceive ourselves, and the truth is not in us.

If we say that we have not sinned, we make Him a liar, and His word is not in us. (I John 1:8,10)

6. Show the prospect that the wages of sin is death. It is the second death stated in Revelation 20:14. Let him read Romans 6:23 with you.

For the wages of sin is death; but the gift of God is eternal life through Jesus Christ our Lord. (Rom. 6:23)

7. Show the prospect that death is eternal punishment in the lake of fire. Let him read Revelation 21:8 with you.

But the fearful, and unbelieving, and the abominable, and murderers, and whoremongers, and sorcerers, and idolaters, and all liars, shall have their part in the lake which burneth with fire and brimstone: which is the second death. (Rev. 21:8)

8. Show the prospect the views of Robert L. Sumner concerning Seventh-Day Adventism. He wrote:

Seventh-day Adventism has a totally false foundation: its understanding of the 2,300 days in Daniel 8:13,14 (1981:3).

Seventh-day Adventism has a totally false, unscriptural teaching of "investigative judgment" (Ibid.:6).

Seventh-day Adventists have a totally false understanding of divine inspiration, equating the writings of Ellen G. White with the Bible! (Ibid.:9)

Here is another serious problem I have with the Seventh-day Adventism: it has a totally false understanding of divine law. It mistakenly teaches that people are still under law during this New Testament dispensation of grace; it repeatedly equates "the law" with "the ten commandments" and it completely disregards the clear teaching as to whom and for whom the law as given (Ibid.:17).

Lead Him to Faith in Jesus Christ

At this point, the prospect might be scared and have second thoughts, and be interested in knowing how he can be saved. Show him God's plan of salvation by using Section A, Chapter IX, of this book. If he claims to be righteous, use Section C. If he claims to be religious, use Section D. But if he is not interested, use Section B.

Appendix E

Dealing With Prospects Who Are Jehovah's Witnesses

Jehovah's Witnesses is one of the fastest growing cult organizations in the world. It is one of the cults listed in *The Kingdom of the Cults* by Dr. Walter Martin.

Their Background

Charles Taze Russell was the founder of the present Jehovah's Witnesses. He was raised in the Congregational Church. He started a Bible study class in 1872, and from this group he organized the present Jehovah's Witnesses (Passantino 1981:50).

Russell was never ordained as a pastor, but his followers called him a pastor. Although Russell claimed to have been ordained, he later admitted in court, "I never was." His title was only "assumed not earned" and he had "never been ordained and [had] no ministerial standing in any religious sect than his own" (Martin 1985:44-46).

While Russell was growing as a public figure in religion, controversy also was growing in his life. He was found to have "lied under oath" about knowing how to read the Greek letters. "He also denied under oath that his wife had divorced him..." (Martin 1981:37,38).

Dr. Martin wrote that "Russell had succeeded in convincing his flock that Jesus referred to him when he spoke of 'a faithful and wise servant, whom his lord hath made ruler over his household, to give them meat in due season' (Matt. 24:25). He explicitly encouraged his followers to look to him as God's sole appointed dispenser of 'present truth' " (1981:38).

But the truth is, "his interpretation of the Bible, not the Bible itself...was to be the supreme authority for every believer" (Martin 1981:38).

Charles Taze Russell was succeeded by a lawyer and judge named Joseph Franklin Rutherford in 1917. Judge Rutherford was a "prolific writer" and a "capable administrator" (Martin 1981). However, like people in the other cults, he failed in all his predictions. Rutherford prophesied "that the millenial reign would arrive within a short period of time." He prophesied that by 1925, the faithful men of Israel would return. But the year 1925 came without the faithful men of Israel (Martin 1981).

There are "many splinter groups that had formed" before Rutherford died in 1942. His successor, Nathan Homer Knorr, was vice president in 1940. Knorr's greatest achievement is the Jehovah's Witnesses' translation of the Bible, called the New World Translation. When Knorr died in 1977, he was succeeded by Frederick W. Franz, who followed the footsteps of his predecessors. He was instrumental in increasing the membership to "over a million members" during his tenure of office. These are the four figures that led the Jehovah's Witnesses to its present organizational success and strength (Passantino 1981:53-55).

Their Beliefs and Doctrines

The Jehovah's Witnesses believe and teach that there is only one God; that Jesus Christ is created by God. They say that Jesus is the Son of God, but that He is not God Himself. He is a mighty god, but not the Almighty God. They also teach that the Holy Spirit is not a person, only an active force of God.

The following are some of the beliefs and doctrines of the Witnesses as quoted by Dr. Martin.

About the Holy Trinity

1. "The doctrine, in belief, is that there are three gods in one: 'God the Father, God the Son, and God the Holy Ghost,' all three equal in power, substance and eternity" (*Let God Be True*, Brooklyn: Watchtower Bible and Tract Society, 1946 ed., p. 100).

2. "The obvious conclusion is, therefore, that satan is the originator of the trinity doctrine" (Ibid.: 101).

3. "...sincere persons who want to know the true God and serve Him find it a bit difficult to love and worship a complicated, freakish-looking, three-headed God" (Ibid.: 102) (Martin 1985:52,53).

About God

1. There is one solitary being from all eternity, Jehovah God, the Creator and Preserver of the Universe and all things visible and invisible (1985:51).

About the Deity of Jesus Christ

1. "...the true Scriptures speak of God's Son, the Word, as 'a god.' He is a 'mighty god,' but not the Almighty God, who is Jehovah" (*The Truth Shall Make You Free,* Brooklyn: Watchtower Bible and Tract Society, 1943, p. 47).

2. "In other words, he was the first and direct creation of Jehovah God" (*The Kingdom Is at Hand,* Brooklyn: Watchtower Bible and Tract Society, 1944, pp. 46,47,49).

3. "...the Bible shows that there is only one God...'greater than His Son.' ...And the Son, as the first born, Only begotten and 'the creation by God,' had a beginning. That the Father is greater and older than the Son is reasonable, easy to understand and is what the Bible teaches" (*From Paradise Lost to Paradise Regained,* Brooklyn: Watchtower Bible and Tract Society, 1958, p. 164).

4. "...Jesus was 'the Son of God.' Not God himself!" (*"The Word" Who Is He?,* Brooklyn Watchtower Bible and Tract Society, p. 20) (1985:53).

About the Holy Spirit

1. "...The holy spirit is the invincible active force of Almighty God that moves his servants to do his will" (*Let God Be True*, p. 108).

2. "As for the 'Holy Spirit,' the so-called 'third person of the Trinity,' we have already seen that it is, not a person, but God's active force" (*The Truth That Leads to Eternal Life*, Brooklyn: Watchtower Bible and Tract Society, 1968, p. 24).

3. "The Scriptures themselves unite to show that God's holy spirit is not a person but is God's active force by which he accomplishes his purpose and executes his will" (*Aid to Bible Understanding*, Brooklyn: Watchtower Bible and Tract Society, 1969, 1971, p. 1543) (1985:53).

About Salvation

1. "Immortality is a reward for faithfulness. It does not come automatically to a human at birth" (*Let God Be True*, p. 74).

2. "Those people of good will today who avail of the provision and who steadfastly abide in this confidence will find Christ Jesus to be their 'everlasting Father' " (Isa. 9:6) (*Let God Be True.*, p. 121).

3. "We have learned that a person could fall away and be judged unfavorably either now or at Armageddon, or during the thousand years of Christ's reign, or at the end of the final test...into everlasting destruction" (*From Paradise Lost to Paradise Regained*, p. 241) (1985:54).

About the Nature and Destiny of Man's Soul

1. "...man is a combination of two things, namely, the 'dust of the ground' and 'the breath of life.' The

combination of these two things (or factors) produced a living soul or creature called man" (1985:68).

2. "So we see that the claim of religionists that man has an immortal soul and therefore differs from the beast is not Scriptural" (Ibid., p. 68).

3. The fact that the human soul is mortal soul can be amply proved by a careful study of the Holy Scriptures. An immortal soul can not die, but God's Word, at Ezekiel 18:4, says concerning humans: 'Behold all souls are mine;...the soul that sinneth it die' " (Ibid., pp. 69,70).

4. "...it is clearly seen that even the man Christ Jesus was mortal. He did not have an immortal soul: Jesus, the human soul, died" (Ibid., p. 71).

5. "Thus it is seen that the serpent (the Devil) is the one that originated the doctrine of the inherent immortality of human souls" (Ibid., 74,75).

6. "The Scriptures show that the destiny of the sinful man is death" (Ibid., p. 75).

7. "...the Holy Scriptures alone offers real hope for those who do seek Jehovah God and strive to follow his ways" (Ibid., p. 75) (1985:56).

Methods of Indoctrination

I would like to incorporate here the methods of operation that the Jehovah's Witnesses use to win the people to their fold and to make more money, as related by William Schnell in his book, *Thirty Years a Watchtower Slave.*

According to Mr. Schnell, a former member of the Jehovah's Witnesses, the Witnesses have developed and perfected seven steps of indoctrination, or brainwashing.

1. Get "the books into the hands of the person" or sell the books to the prospect, on behalf of the Watchtower Society.

2. Do a "back call" or follow-up, "to encourage a purchaser to study the book he had acquired."

3. "Get the person called on to agree to a weekly study...of the books he had acquired."

4. Do "the area book study," which leads their prospect into the area of brainwashing and indoctrination.

5. "Lead the person into a wider area of Watchtower indoctrination," to eradicate the concept of salvation by Jesus Christ from their hearts and minds. Lead them to find salvation in the "City of refuge, which was God's Organization."

6. "Attend Service meetings and publish in harmony with organization instructions." Teach the person how to present the books, how to conduct back calls, how to conduct book studies, and how to get contributions of money.

7. "The climax of the entire procedure is by persuading the victims to become baptized and initiated into the Theocracy." The rite of baptism is used only as an "outward sign of official entry into God's Organization, or city of refuge."

As long as he remains in good standing, "he is in the city of refuge! He will escape Armageddon" (Schnell 1971:121-129).

Their missions or motives, according to Mr. Schnell, with the Jehovah's Witnesses referring to Matthew

28:19-20 as the basis of their mission, is to make money by preaching the "Gospel of the Kingdom." He wrote:

> The Watchtower already in 1922 had set out to "preach the Gospel of the Kingdom." But they did not do so to disciple the nations, that is, to bring them to Christ as brethrens, or equals before the throne of grace. No, they did so to gain money to make the Organization strong and powerful, and to gain prestige for the Organization. With "feigned words" they "made merchandise" of men (1971:162).

How to Deal With the Jehovah's Witness

If you meet a Jehovah's Witness while you're out soul winning, don't allow him to control the conversation. Before he starts presenting or reciting a list of Bible verses, ask him to allow you to first read some Bible verses. He may reluctantly agree. So start by reading:

About God the Father

1. Show the prospect that there is only one God, and no one beside Him. Let him read Isaiah 43:10 with you.

> *Ye are My witnesses, saith the Lord, and My servant whom I have chosen; that ye may know and believe Me, and understand that I am He: before Me there was no God formed, neither shall there be after Me.* (Isa. 43:10)

> *I am the Lord, and there is none else, there is no God beside Me: I girded thee, though thou hast not known Me.* (Isa. 45:5)

Dealing With Prospects Who Are Jehovah's Witnesses

2. Show the prospect that the Father is the only true God as well as the Son Jesus Christ whom He sent. Let him read John 17:3 with you.

And this is life eternal, that they might know Thee the only true God, and Jesus Christ, whom Thou hast sent. (John 17:3)

About the Son Jesus Christ

1. Show the prospect that Jesus Christ was with God in the beginning and that He was God. Show him that He was the Creator of everything, and without Him nothing was created. Let him read John 1:1-3 with you.

In the beginning was the Word, and the Word was with God, and the Word was God.

The same was in the beginning with God.

All things were made by Him; and without Him was not any thing made that was made. (John 1:1-3)

To have a clearer view of these verses, let's compare these with the verses from The Living Bible.

Before anything else existed, there was Christ, with God. He has always been alive and is Himself God.

He created everything there is—nothing exists that He didn't make. (John 1:1-3 TLB)

2. Show the prospect that Jesus Christ is the Creator of everything that was created. Let him read Colossians 1:15 and 16 with you.

Who is the image of the invisible God, the firstborn of every creature:

For by Him were all things created, that are in heaven, and that are in earth, visible and invisible, whether they be thrones, or dominions, or principalities, or powers: all things were created by Him, and for Him. (Col. 1:15,16)

The prospect might say that Jesus Christ was created as stated in verse 15. Let us look at the verses from The Living Bible. This is what they say:

Christ is the exact likeness of the unseen God. He existed before God made anything at all, and, in fact,

Christ Himself is the Creator who made everything in heaven and earth, the things we can see and the things we can't, the spirit world with its kings and kingdoms, its rulers and authorities; all were made by Christ for His own use and glory. (Col. 1:15,16 TLB)

3. Show the prospect that Jesus Christ existed before Abraham was born. Let him read John 8:58 with you.

Jesus said unto them, Verily, verily, I say unto you, Before Abraham was, I am. (John 8:58)

4. Show the prospect that Jesus Christ was the spiritual Rock that followed the Israelites in the wilderness when they came out of Egypt. Let him read First Corinthians 10:4 with you.

And did all drink the same spiritual drink: for they drank of that spiritual Rock that followed them: and that Rock was Christ. (I Cor. 10:4)

5. Show the prospect that Jesus Christ, the Son of the living God, became man and dwelt among His people. Let him read John 1:14 with you.

And the Word was made flesh, and dwelt among us, (and we beheld His glory, the glory as of the only begotten of the Father,) full of grace and truth. (John 1:14)

6. Show the prospect that God the Father testified to the fact that Jesus is God. Let him read Hebrews 1:8 with you.

But unto the Son He saith, Thy throne, O God, is for ever and ever: a sceptre of righteousness is the sceptre of Thy kingdom. (Heb 1:8)

7. Show the prospect that Jesus Christ is the Son of God and the true God. Let him read First John 5:20 with you.

And we know that the Son of God is come, and hath given us an understanding, that we may know Him that is true, and we are in Him that is true, even in His Son Jesus Christ. This is the true God, and eternal life. (I John 5:20)

8. Show the prospect that the apostle Thomas confessed Jesus Christ as his Lord and his God. Let him read John 20:28 with you.

And Thomas answered and said unto Him, My Lord and my God. (John 20:28)

9. Show the prospect that before Jesus Christ became a man, Isaiah prophesied that He was God. Let him read Isaiah 9:6 with you.

For unto us a child is born, unto us a son is given: and the government shall be upon His shoulder: and His name shall be called Wonderful, Counsellor, The mighty God, The everlasting Father, the Prince of Peace. (Isa. 9:6)

At this point, the prospect might say that Jesus is inferior to Jehovah God. He could say that Jesus Christ is only a mighty God, not the Almighty God. Show the prospect that Jesus Christ is Almighty God. Let him read Revelation 1:8 with you.

I am Alpha and Omega, the beginning and the ending, saith the Lord, which is, and which was, and which is to come, the Almighty. (Rev. 1:8)

10. Show the prospect that the gospel of truth is hidden to non-believers. The devil has blinded the eyes and minds of the non-believers so they cannot see the light from Jesus Christ. Let him read Second Corinthians 4:3 and 4 with you.

But if our gospel be hid, it is hid to them that are lost:

In whom the god of this world hath blinded the minds of them which believe not, lest the light of the glorious gospel of Christ, who is the image of God, should shine unto them. (II Cor. 4:3,4)

11. Show the prospect that non-believers are the children of the devil. Let him read John 8:44 with you.

Ye are of your father the devil, and the lusts of your father ye will do. He was a murderer from the beginning, and abode not in the truth, because there is no truth in him. When he speaketh a lie, he speaketh of his own: for he is a liar, and the father of it. (John 8:44)

12. Show the prospect that only those who believe and receive Jesus Christ as their personal divine Lord and Savior will become children of God. Let him read John 1:12 with you.

But as many as received Him, to them gave He power to become the sons of God, even to them that believe on His name. (John 1:12)

13. Show the prospect that there are false prophets as well as false teachers and preachers. Let him read Matthew 7:15 and Second Corinthians 11:13 and 14 with you.

Beware of false prophets, which come to you in sheep's clothing, but inwardly they are ravening wolves. (Matt. 7:15)

For such are false apostles, deceitful workers, transforming themselves into the apostles of Christ.

And no marvel; for Satan himself is transformed into an angel of light. (II Cor. 11:13,14)

About the Holy Spirit

The Holy Spirit is a divine person, the third person in the Trinity, and He is God. The Bible clearly states that the Holy Spirit is God.

1. Show the prospect that the Holy Spirit can perform things. Let him read Genesis 1:2 with you.

And the earth was without form and void; and darkness was upon the face of the deep. And the spirit of God moved upon the face of the waters. (Gen. 1:2)

2. Show the prospect that the Holy Spirit can talk. Let him read Acts 13:2 and Revelation 2:7 with you.

As they ministered to the Lord, and fasted, the Holy Ghost said, Separate Me Barnabas and Saul for the work whereunto I have called them. (Acts 13:2)

He that hath an ear, let him hear what the Spirit saith unto the churches... (Rev. 2:7)

3. Show the prospect that the Holy Spirit can testify. Let him read John 15:26 with you.

But when the Comforter is come, whom I will send unto you from the Father, even the Spirit of truth, which proceedeth from the Father, He shall testify of Me. (John 15:26)

4. Show the prospect that the Holy Spirit can command. Let him read Acts 8:29 with you.

Then the Spirit said unto Philip, Go near, and join thyself to this chariot. (Acts 8:29)

5. Show the prospect that the Holy Spirit can guide. Let him read John 16:13 with you.

Howbeit when He, the Spirit of truth, is come, He will guide you into all truth: for He shall not speak of

Himself; but whatsoever He shall hear, that shall He speak: and He will shew you things to come. (John 16:13)

6. Show the prospect that the Holy Spirit can and will dwell in the hearts of all who truly believe and receive Jesus Christ as their personal divine Lord and Savior. Let him read John 14:17 with you.

Even the Spirit of truth; whom the world cannot receive, because it seeth Him not, neither knoweth Him: but ye know Him; for He dwelleth with you, and shall be in you. (John 14:17)

7. Show the prospect that the Holy Spirit is Himself God. Let him read Acts 5:3 and 4 with you.

But Peter said, Ananias, why hath Satan filled thine heart to lie to the Holy Ghost, and to keep back part of the price of the land?

Whiles it remained, was it not thine own? and after it was sold, was it not in thine own power? why hast thou conceived this thing in thine heart? thou hast not lied unto men, but unto God. (Acts 5:3,4)

About the Trinity

Christians believe that there are three persons in one God, not three Gods in one, as the non-believers always say to ridicule the Christians.

1. Show the prospect that there are three persons "that bear record in heaven," and are one. Let him read First John 5:7 with you.

For there are three that bear record in heaven, the Father, the Word, and the Holy Ghost: and these three are one. (I John 5:7)

2. Show the prospect that before Jesus Christ went back to be with the Father, He commissioned His disciples to win and to baptize the people of all nations in the name of these three persons. Let him read Matthew 28:18 and 19 with you.

And Jesus came and spake unto them, saying, All power is given unto Me in heaven and in earth.

Go ye therefore, and teach all nations, baptizing them in the name of the Father, and of the Son, and of the Holy Ghost. (Matt. 28:18,19)

3. Show the prospect that Jesus Christ Himself said that He and the Father are one. Let him read John 10:30 with you.

I and my Father are one. (John 10:30)

4. Show the prospect that the God who created heaven and earth in Genesis 1:1 is the God the Father, God the Son, and God the Holy Spirit. Let him read Genesis 1:26; 3:22 and 11:6 and 7 with you.

And God said, Let Us make man in Our image, after Our likeness: and let them have dominion over the fish of the sea, and over the fowl of the air, and over the cattle, and over all the earth, and over every creeping thing that creepeth upon the earth. (Gen. 1:26)

And the Lord God said, Behold, the man is become as one of Us, to know good and evil: and now, lest he put forth his hand, and take also of the tree of life, and eat, and live forever. (Gen. 3:22)

And the Lord said, Behold, the people is one and they have all one language; and this they begin to do: and now nothing will be restrained from them, which they have imagined to do.

Go to, let Us go down, and there confound their language, that they may not understand one another's speech. (Gen. 11:6,7)

About Salvation

As a religious people, the Jehovah's Witnesses' main objective is the salvation of their souls. They must do everything they know to achieve their objective, the salvation of their souls.

1. Show the prospect that all are sinners, including youself, the prospect and everybody. Let him read Romans 3:23 with you.

For all have sinned, and come short of the glory of God. (Rom. 3:23)

2. Show the prospect that the wages of sin is death. Let him read Romans 6:23 with you.

For the wages of sin is death; but the gift of God is eternal life through Jesus Christ our Lord. (Rom. 6:23)

3. Show the prospect that, as a sinner, he is spiritually dead. That means, he is separated from God. It is the second death. Let him read Revelation 21:8 with you.

But the fearful, and unbelieving, and the abominable, and murderers, and whoremongers, and sorcerers, and idolaters, and all liars, shall have their part in the lake which burneth with fire and brimstone: which is the second death. (Rev. 21:8)

At this point, the prospect might be scared and ask you what he should do in order to be saved.

Lead Him to Faith in Jesus Christ

Lead the prospect to believe and accept Jesus Christ as his personal divine Lord and Savior. Show him the way of salvation by using Section A of Chapter IX in this book. If he claims to be religious, use Section D. If he claims to be righteous, use Section C. If he is not interested in the salvation of his soul, use Section B.

Appendix F

Dealing With Prospects Who Are of the Iglesia ni Cristo (Manalo)

The Iglesia ni Cristo, popularly known as Manalista, is one of the fastest growing, independent non-Protestant and non-Roman Catholic religious sect in the Philippines. They call themselves Iglesia, but they now use Protestant terms, having defined them to fit their doctrines: evangelism, Christian, evangelical, etc. As a matter of fact, they named their school, "New Era Evangelical College."

The Iglesia ni Christo (Manalo) pride themselves on their great numbers and huge chapels. The Editorial of the *Pasugo,* July 1964, as quoted by Dr. Gabriel, says:

> From one beginning with Brother Felix Manalo, the Church of Christ, both in members and in material blessings, count by the millions. In point of membership, we present not our testimony, but that of the metropolitan newspapers, reporting of people that attended the funeral of our late Brother—more than a million and a half, and these came from Luzon...
>
> In point of material blessings, we point to many concrete chapels worth millions of pesos, complete with architectural designs, and the chapels worth lots of million pesos too. (Gabriel 1964:7).

But the Bible says: "Enter ye in at the strait gate: for wide is the gate, and broad is the way, that leadeth to destruction, and many there be which go in thereat: because strait is the gate, and narrow is the way, which leadeth unto life, and few there be that find it" (Matt. 7:13,14).

Their Background

The Iglesia ni Cristo (Manalo) was founded by Felix Manalo in 1914, after he was "disfellowshiped by the Seventh Day Adventist Church." Manalo, a Roman Catholic in name, was converted to a Protestant sect. He was trained under the Presbyterian Church and served several Evangelical churches, such as the Methodist, the Church of Christ disciples, the Christian Alliance, the Presbyterian and the Seventh Day Adventist Church. (Gabriel 1981:3-6).

The Iglesia ni Cristo (Manalo) was registered on July 27, 1914, and was reconstituted and amended in July 29, 1946. The articles of incorporation are a *Corporacion Unipersonal* or Corporation Sole. "This meant that Manalo as 'head of the Society,' he takes charge and is the administrator of all the properties and states of the Society," says Dr. Tuggy (1976:46). It is a one-man corporation, a corporation administered and owned by only one person. It "consists of one person only and his successors" (Gabriel 1981:20).

The Iglesia ni Cristo suffered two schisms, one led by Mr. Teofilo Ora, 1922 and one led by Dr. Melanio Gabriel, Jr., in 1979. After the Ora rebellion and after the Rosita Trillanes case in 1922, Felix Manalo introduced a new doctrine, the "Sugo" doctrine, or God's messenger of the last days, to establish supreme authority over the Iglesia ni Cristo. This is how Dr. Tuggy describes the situation:

Thus, in 1922 Manalo faced a crucial challenge to his authority within the church. It was about this time that Manalo introduced a new doctrine which was to become the cornerstone of the entire doctrinal structure of the Iglesia ni Cristo. The doctrine affirms Manalo's position as "Sugo" or "God's Messenger" in fulfillment of the prophecy in Revelation 7:1-3. It provided a firm doctrinal foundation for his authority. The emergence of this doctrine at this particular time could hardly have been coincidental. It is reasonable to assume that it grew out of Manalo's determination to stablish supreme authority over the Iglesia ni Cristo (1976:57,58).

Dr. Tuggy further states that Manalo claimed to be the angel ascending from the far east in Revelation 7:2, "who began his ascent on July 27, 1914," to establish the Iglesia ni Cristo in the Philippines, the far east of the prophecy (1976:59).

With this new doctrine, Manalo asserted his authority over the Iglesia ni Cristo. Dr. Tuggy wrote:

> With Manalo's authority clearly established by the "Angel" doctrine, disloyalty firmly purged from the ranks, and all property owned by the Supreme Head, the church was ready for its first period of really rapid growth. The Iglesia was never again seriously threatened by schism (1976:59).

However, the Iglesia ni Cristo suffered its greatest schism in August 3, 1979, led by Dr. Melanio Gabriel, Jr., who organized the "Love of Christ Fellowship" in Metro Manila, Philippines. Dr. Gabriel is a doctor of medicine by profession. He was one of the higher officers of the Iglesia ni Cristo under Manalo. In April of 1979, Dr. Gabriel was converted and received Jesus Christ as his personal Lord and Savior. After his conversion, he started giving testimonies about his experiences with the Lord. With the help of other Christians, he organized prayer meetings and Bible studies. As a result, many were converted. He claimed that one third of the Iglesia ni Cristo in Metro Manila joined him in the Love of Christ Fellowship.

The Iglesia ni Cristo (Manalo) tends to appeal primarily to the uneducated, to members of the Roman Catholic Church, and to members of the Evangelical churches who are still immature in their faith.

Felix Manalo died on April 12, 1963, at the age of 77. He was succeeded by his son Erano Manalo.

Their Beliefs and Doctrines

The beliefs and doctrines of the Iglesia ni Cristo (Manalo) have been a bitter condemnation of all the Christian groups, in order to lure them to their own fold as the only true Church of Christ.

They believe and teach that there is only one God; there is no Trinity; Jesus Christ is not God; the Holy Spirit is not God, but "is the power sent by the Father in the name of Christ"; Jesus Christ is the founder of the Iglesia ni Cristo (Manalo) in the Philippines; the Iglesia ni Cristo (Manalo) "is the only means of man's salvation in the Christian era" (Santiago, *Pasugo* May-June 1986:40,41); Manalo is the "Sugo," God's messenger of the last days, the angel, and the ravenous bird from the east.

How to Deal With the Iglesia ni Cristo (Manalo)

The soul winner must be familiar with the beliefs and doctrines of the Iglesia ni Cristo (Manalo). They always challenge you to a debate with their debater. Do not accept the challenge. Challenge the prospect instead to study the Bible with you and to discover what the Bible says. For sure, the prospect will not accept the challenge, but encourage him to know the truth, for the truth will make him free.

The Truth About God

The Iglesia ni Cristo (Manalo) believed in the "Absolute Oneness of God." This is how Mr. Santiago described their beliefs:

The Iglesia ni Cristo believes in the one and only true God, the Father, taught by our Lord Jesus Christ and His apostles (John 17:3,1; 1 Corinthians 8:6). The Bible teaches that the true God is a Spirit (John 4:24), and being a Spirit He has no bones (Luke 24:39).

The absolute oneness of God does not consist of three divine persons. The Bible indeed speaks of the Father, the Son and the Holy Spirit but it states also clearly and categorically which of the three is the true God (*Pasugo* May-June 1986:39).

It is true that there is only one God. But the Bible also teaches that there are three persons in one God.

1. Show the prospect that God in Genesis 1:1,26 and 3:22 means God the Father, God the Son, and God the Holy Spirit. Let him read Genesis 1:1,26; 3:22 and 11:6 and 7 with you.

*In the beginning **God** created the heaven and the earth.* (Gen. 1:1)

*And God said, **Let Us make man in Our image, after Our likeness**...* (Gen. 1:26)

*And the Lord God said, Behold, **the man is become as one of Us**...* (Gen. 3:22)

And the Lord said...

Go to, let Us go down... (Gen. 11:6,7)

2. Show the prospect that there are three persons "that bear record in heaven" and are one. Let him read First John 5:7 with you.

> *For there are three that bear record in heaven, the Father, the Word [Jesus Christ], and the Holy Ghost: and these three are one.* (I John 5:7)

3. Show the prospect that Jesus Christ Himself said that He and the Father are one. Let him read John 10:30 with you.

> *I and My Father are one.* (John 10:30)

4. Show the prospect that before Jesus Christ went back to be with the Father, He commissioned His disciples to win the lost souls and to baptize them in the name of these three persons. Let him read Matthew 28:18 and 19 with you.

> *And Jesus came and spake unto them, saying, All power is given unto Me in heaven and in earth.*
>
> *Go ye therefore, and teach all nations, baptizing them in the name of the Father, and of the Son, and of the Holy Ghost.* (Matt. 28:18,19)

About Jesus Christ the Son

The Iglesia ni Cristo believe and teach that Jesus Christ is just a human being. This is how Mr. Santiago described Him:

> The Iglesia ni Cristo believes in Jesus Christ, the Son of God (Matthew 3:17): the one and only Savior given by God (Acts 13:23): Christ is the sole mediator between God and men (1 Timothy 2:5) and the only way to God (John 14:6).
>
> Christ is not a God-Man. He is man in nature according to His own testimony (John 8:40) and

the teachings of His apostles (1 Timothy 2:5; Matthew 1:18) (*Pasugo* May-June 1986:40).

Ask the prospect to show you where in the Bible he can find a verse that says, Jesus Christ is not God. Remember that God is powerful and can transform Himself to a human being, but a man cannot become a God.

1. Show the prospect that it is true Jesus Christ possessed human nature, but that it is also true He possessed a divine nature. He is God, but He became a man. Let the prospect read John 1:1,2 and 14 with you.

In the beginning was the Word, and the Word was with God, and the Word was God.

The same was in the beginning with God. (John 1:1,2)

And the Word was made flesh, and dwelt among us, (and we beheld His glory, the glory as of the only begotten of the Father,) full of grace and truth. (John 1:14)

To have a clearer view of these verses, let's compare these with the verses from The Living Bible.

Before anything else existed, there was Christ, with God. He has always been alive and is Himself God. (John 1:1,2 TLB)

And Christ became a human being and lived here on earth among us and was full of loving forgiveness and truth. And some of us have seen His glory—the glory of the only Son of the heavenly Father! (John 1:14 TLB)

2. Show the prospect that Jesus Christ is the Creator of everything that was created. Let him read John 1:3 and Colossians 1:16 with you.

All things were made by Him [Jesus Christ]; *and without Him was not any thing made that was made.* (John 1:3)

For by Him [Jesus Christ] *were all things created, that are in heaven, and that are in earth, visible and invisible, whether they be thrones, or dominions, or principalities, or powers: all things were created by Him, and for Him.* (Col. 1:16)

The prospect might reason out that Jesus Christ was a created being, using verse 15, which says: "Who is the image of the invisible God, the firstborn of every creature." This verse does not imply that Jesus Christ was created. Compare it with the verse from The Living Bible: "Christ is the exact likeness of the unseen God. He existed before God made anything at all..." (Col. 1:15 TLB).

3. Show the prospect that Jesus Christ existed before Abraham was born. Let him read John 8:58 with you.

Jesus said unto them, Verily, verily, I say unto you, Before Abraham was, I am. (John 8:58)

4. Show the prospect that Jesus Christ was the spiritual Rock that followed the Israelites in the wilderness when they came out of Egypt. Let him read First Corinthians 10:4 with you.

And did all drink of the same spiritual drink: for they drank of that spiritual Rock that followed them: and that Rock was Christ. (I Cor. 10:4)

5. Show the prospect that God the Father testified to the fact that Jesus Christ is God. Let him read Hebrews 1:8 with you.

But unto the Son He saith, Thy throne, O God, is for ever and ever: a sceptre of righteousness is the sceptre of Thy kingdom. (Heb. 1:8)

Compare this verse with the one in The Living Bible. It says:

But of His Son He says, "Your kingdom, O God, will last forever and ever; its commands are always just and right." (Heb. 1:8 TLB)

6. Show the prospect that Jesus Christ, the Son of God, is true God. Let him read First John 5:20 with you.

And we know that the Son of God is come, and hath given us an understanding, that we may know Him that is true, and we are in Him that is true, even in His Son Jesus Christ. This is the true God, and eternal life.

7. Show the prospect that the apostle Thomas confessed Jesus Christ as his Lord and his God. Let him read John 20:28 with you.

And Thomas answered and said unto Him, My Lord and my God. (John 20:28)

8. Show the prospect that before Jesus Christ became a man, as was prophesied by Isaiah, He was (and is) God. Let him read Isaiah 9:6 with you.

For unto us a child is born, unto us a son is given: and the government shall be upon His shoulder: and The everlasting Father, The Prince of Peace. (Isa. 9:6)

At this point, the prospect might say that Jesus Christ is inferior to Jehovah God. He could say that Jesus Christ is only mighty God, and not the Almighty God.

9. Show the prospect that Jesus Christ is the Almighty God. Let him read Revelation 1:8 with you.

*I am Alpha and Omega, the beginning and the ending, saith the Lord, which is, and which was, and which is to come, the **Almighty**.* (Rev. 1:8)

At this point, the prospect might reason that this verse refers to the Father and not to the Son. Let the prospect read Revelation 1:10,11,17 and 18 with you.

I was in the Spirit on the Lord's day, and heard behind me a great voice, as of a trumpet,

Saying, I am Alpha and Omega, the first and the last... (Rev. 1:10,11)

*And when I saw Him, I fell at His feet as dead. And He laid His right hand upon me, saying unto me, Fear not; **I am the first and the last**:*

I am He that liveth, and was dead; and, behold, I am alive for evermore... (Rev. 1:17,18)

10. Show the prospect that the gospel of truth is hidden to non-believers. The devil has blinded the eyes and minds of non-believers so they cannot see the light from Jesus Christ. Let him read Second Corinthians 4:3 and 4 with you.

But if our gospel be hid, it is hid to them that are lost:

In whom the god of this world hath blinded the minds of them which believe not, lest the light of the glorious gospel of Christ, who is the image of God, should shine unto them. (II Cor. 4:3,4)

11. Show the prospect that the non-believers are the children of the devil. Let him read John 8:44 with you.

Ye are of your father the devil, and the lusts of your father ye will do. He was a murderer from the beginning, and abode not in the truth, because there is no truth in him. When he speaketh a lie, he speaketh of his own: for he is a liar, and the father of it. (John 8:44)

12. Show the prospect that only those who believe and receive Jesus Christ as their personal divine Lord and Savior will become children of God. Let him read John 1:12 with you.

But as many as received Him, to them gave He power to become the sons of God, even to them that believe on His name. (John 1:12)

13. Show the prospect that there are false prophets as well as false teachers and preachers. Let him read Matthew 7:15 and Second Corinthians 11:13 and 14 with you.

Beware of false prophets, which come to you in sheep's clothing, but inwardly they are ravening wolves. (Matt. 7:15)

For such are false apostles, deceitful workers, transforming themselves into the apostles of Christ.

And no marvel; for Satan himself is transformed into an angel of light. (II Cor. 11:13,14)

Dealing With Prospects Who Are of the Iglesia ni Cristo

14. Show the prospect that Jesus Christ was in His glory with the Father before the world was made. Let him read John 17:5 with you.

And now, O Father, glorify Thou Me with Thine own self with the glory which I had with Thee before the world was. (John 17:5)

15. Show the prospect that Jesus Christ is equal with God and is God. Let him read Philippians 2:5-8 with you.

Let this mind be in you, which was also in Christ Jesus:

Who, being in the form of God, thought it not robbery to be equal with God:

But made Himself of no reputation, and took upon Him the form of a servant, and was made in the likeness of men:

And being found in fashion as a man, He humbled Himself, and became obedient unto death, even the death of the cross. (Phil. 2:5-8)

16. Show the prospect that the Jews wanted to kill Jesus Christ when He said that God was His Father. Let him read John 5:17 and 18 with you.

But Jesus answered them, My Father worketh hitherto, and I work.

Therefore the Jews sought the more to kill Him, because He not only had broken the sabbath, but said also that God was His Father, making Himself equal with God. (John 5:17,18)

17. Show the prospect that not everyone who says "Lord, Lord" will enter the Kingdom of God. Let him read Matthew 7:21 with you.

Not every one that saith unto Me, Lord, Lord, shall enter into the kingdom of heaven; but he that doeth the will of My Father which is in heaven. (Matt. 7:21)

About the Holy Spirit

The Iglesia ni Cristo (Manalo) believe and teach that the Holy Spirit is not a person and not God. He is only a power sent by the Father and by Jesus Christ. This is their belief and teaching about the Holy Spirit, according to Santiago:

> The Church of Christ believes in the Holy Spirit. This is the power (Acts 1:8) sent by the Father in the name of Christ, to teach and remind His messengers of all the things that Christ said (John 14:26).
>
> The Holy Spirit is also sent by Christ to help us in our weaknesses and infirmities (John 15:26; Romans 8:26) (*Pasugo* May-June 1986:40).

The Holy Spirit is a divine person, the third person in the Trinity, and He is God. The Bible clearly states that the Holy Spirit is God.

1. Show the prospect that the Holy Spirit can perform things. Let him read Genesis 1:2 with you.

*And the earth was without form, and void; and darkness was upon the face of the deep. And the **Spirit of God** moved upon the face of the waters.* (Gen. 1:2)

2. Show the prospect that the Holy Spirit can talk. Let him read Acts 13:2 and Revelation 2:7 with you.

Dealing With Prospects Who Are of the Iglesia ni Cristo

As they ministered to the Lord, and fasted, the Holy Ghost said, Separate Me Barnabas and Saul for the work whereunto I have called them. (Acts 13:2)

He that hath an ear, let him hear what the Spirit saith unto the churches... (Rev. 2:7)

3. Show the prospect that the Holy Spirit can testify. Let him read John 15:26 with you.

But when the Comforter is come, whom I will send unto you from the Father, even the Spirit of truth, which proceedeth from the Father, He shall testify of Me. (John 15:26)

4. Show the prospect that the Holy Spirit can command. Let him read Acts 8:29 with you.

Then the Spirit said unto Philip, Go near, and join thyself to this chariot. (Acts 8:29)

5. Show the prospect that the Holy Spirit can guide. Let him read John 16:13 with you.

Howbeit when He, the Spirit of truth, is come, He will guide you into all truth: for He shall not speak of Himself; but whatsoever He shall hear, that shall He speak: and He will show you things to come. (John 16:13)

6. Show the prospect that the Holy Spirit can and will dwell in the hearts of all who truly believe and receive Jesus Christ as their personal divine Lord and Savior. Let him read John 14:17 with you.

Even the Spirit of truth; whom the world cannot receive, because it seeth Him not, neither knoweth

Him: but ye know Him; for He dwelleth with you, and shall be in you. (John 14:17)

7. Show the prospect that the Holy Spirit is Himself God. Let him read Acts 5:3 and 4 with you.

But Peter said, Ananias, why hath satan filled thine heart to lie to the Holy Ghost, and to keep back part of the price of the land?

Whiles it remained, was it not thine own? and after it was sold, was it not in thine own power? why hast thou conceived this thing in thine heart? thou hast not lied unto men, but unto God. (Acts 5:3,4)

About the Church

Felix Manalo claimed that Jesus Christ established His Church based on Matthew 16:18, but that it was non-existent when the apostles died. It was only in July 27, 1914, that Jesus Christ re-established the Iglesia ni Cristo in the Philippines. "Si Cristo ang nagtayo ng Iglesia ni Cristo sa Pilipinas" (Pan-doctrina 1980:15).

1. Show the prospect that in the articles of incorporation, which were registered in July 27, 1914, and reconstituted in July 29, 1946, it is stated that Felix Manalo was the founder of the Iglesia ni Cristo in the Philippines. It says: "Que los *fundadores* de esta asociacion, son; *Felix Manalo*, domiciliado en Tagig, Rizal, I. F."

Felix Manalo claimed that the Iglesia ni Cristo (Manalo), founded by a man, Jesus Christ, in the Philippines, is the only true church. He said that outside the Iglesia ni Cristo (Manalo) there is no salvation.

2. Show the prospect that the church founded by Jesus Christ, the God who became a man, is the true church. Let him read, with you, the Bible verses to prove that the Church of Christ, the Christ who is God, is the only true church. They are the following:

Acts 20:28

*Take heed therefore unto yourselves, and to all the flock, over the which the Holy Ghost hath made you overseers, to feed the **church of God**, which **He hath purchased with His own blood**.*

I Corinthians 1:2

*Unto the **church of God** which is at Corinth, to them that are sanctified in Christ Jesus, called to be saints, with all that in every place call upon the name of Jesus Christ our Lord, both theirs and ours.*

I Corinthians 11:16

*But if any man seen to be contentious, we have no such custom, neither the **churches of God**.*

I Corinthians 11:22

*What? have ye not houses to eat and to drink in? or despise ye the **church of God**, and shame them that have not? What shall I say to you? shall I praise you in this? I praise you not.*

I Corinthians 15:9

*For I am the least of the apostles, that am not meet to be called an apostle, because I persecuted the **church of God**.*

I Thessalonians 2:14

*For ye, brethren, became followers of the **churches of God** which in Judea are in Christ Jesus: for ye have suffered like things of your own countrymen, even as they have of the Jews.*

II Thessalonians 1:4

*So that we ourselves glory in you in the **churches of God** for your patience and faith in all your persecutions and tribulations that ye endure.*

I Timothy 3:5

*(For if a man know not how to rule his own house, how shall he take care of the **church of God**?)*

These verses show that Jesus Christ, who established His Church, is God. So every local congregation or local church that believes and accepts Jesus Christ as their personal divine Lord and Savior is the true church established by Jesus Christ.

About Felix Manalo

The Iglesia ni Cristo (Manalo) believe that Felix Manalo alone can interpret the Bible, and that he alone will decide what the followers should believe and do. This is how Dr. Sanders described the situation:

> Since Felix Manalo founded this sect he has exercised dictatorial powers therein. He is its "Supreme Pastor." He decides how the Bible should be interpreted, what the members should believe, how they should vote, the manner in

which the "church" money should be spent and all properties administered. The "Church" is a corporation and Manalo is the head of the corporation. He therefore acts like a pope, being a "formidable rival of the Roman Pontiff." The government is totalitarian and not democratic being akin to Roman Catholicism in this respect.

The apostle Paul warned the Christians at Corith against their giving allegiance to a man, 1 Cor. 1:2. Our faith and allegiance should always be to Jesus Christ who for the Christian should have "the preeminence in all things," Col. 1:18 (Sanders nd:3).

Felix Manalo claimed that he was *sent* by God to be the messenger of the last days, and his followers believed him. Mr. Catabay says:

> One of the doctrines which we believe in, but unfortunately is misunderstood or unknown to many, concerns God's messenger in these last days...
>
> The importance of God's messenger is clear:
>
> *Jesus answered and said to them, "This is the work of God, that you believe in Him whom He sent"* (John 6:29 NKJ) (Catabay *Pasugo* May-June 1986:24).

In this particular verse, Jesus refers to Himself as the one sent whom we must believe concerning the "everlasting life, which the Son of man shall give unto you..." (John 6:27). It's not Manalo, or anybody, but Jesus Christ.

1. Show the prospect that in the same chapter Jesus talked about everlasting life. He also said that He

was the one sent by God. Let the prospect read John 6:38 and 39 with you.

For I came down from heaven, not to do Mine own will, but the will of Him that sent Me.

And this is the Father's will which hath sent Me, that of all which He hath given Me I should lose nothing, but should raise it up again at the last day. (John 6:38,39)

Felix Manalo claimed that he was the bird of prey from the "Far East," the man who does God's biddings. "The one sent or called by God...will emerge from the Far East." This is how Mr. Catabay described it:

Why do we believe in the commission of Brother Felix Manalo as God's messenger in these last days? Was he sent by God? It is well to remember that being sent is tantamount to being called by God. And one of the means by which God sends or calls His messenger is by prophecy. Here is what the prophet Isaiah said concerning God's messenger in these last days:

Calling a bird of prey from the east, the man who executes My counsel, from a far country. Indeed I have spoken it; I will also bring it to pass. I have purposed it; I will also do it (Isa. 46:11 NKJ) (*Pasugo* May-June 1986:25).

In this verse, however, the bird of prey is not Felix Manalo, but Cyrus of Persia.

2. Show the prospect that Manalo made a grievous mistake by claiming to be the bird of prey. Let

him read the same verse Isaiah 46:11, from The Living Bible with you. It says:

I will call that swift bird of prey from the east—that man Cyrus from far away. And he will come and do My bidding. I have said I would do it and I will. (Is. 46:11 TLB)

In corroboration with The Living Bible, *The Wycliffe Bible Commentary* says:

The ravenous bird and the man who executes God's counsel is of course, Cyrus of Anshon, the province of Persia (1962:642).

Realizing now that the bird of prey is not Manalo, but Cyrus, the followers then say that Manalo "was likened to a bird of prey of the east." This is how Mr. Catabay described their beliefs:

This prophecy of Isaiah concerns a man from the far country. He was likened to a bird of prey from the east. God Himself guaranteed the fulfillment of this prophecy: "I have spoken it; I will also bring it to pass. I have purposed it; I will also do it," he said.

The one sent or called by God, including his offspring or descendants, will emerge from the Far East. They are recognized by God as His sons and daughters from the ends of the earth.

Fear not, for I am with you; I will bring your descendants from the east, and gather you from the west; I will say to the north, 'Give them up!' And to the south, 'Do not keep them back!' Bring My sons from afar, and My daughters from the ends of the earth. (Is. 43:5-6 NKJ)...

The prophecy specified—Far East—and the time element involved—ends of the earth (*Pasugo* May-June 1986:25).

Felix Manalo claimed that the east mentioned in verse 5 is the Philippines, that the children are the Filipinos and that the "ends of the earth" is the end of time or the last days.

3. Show the prospect that the east is Babylon and God was telling Cyrus (not Manalo) to bring back His children, the Israelites, to Israel. The Israelites were scattered to the farthest corners of the earth (not the end of time), during the Babylonian captivity. Let him read Isaiah 43:5 and 6 from The Living Bible with you.

Don't be afraid, for I am with you. I will gather you from east and west,

from north and south. I will bring My sons and daughters back to Israel from the farthest corners of the earth. (Is. 43:5,6 TLB)

4. Show the prospect that in verse 3, God paid Cyrus a ransom for the release of the Israelites, who were captives. Let him read Isaiah 43:3 with you from The Living Bible.

For I am the Lord your God, your Savior, the Holy One of Israel. I gave Egypt and Ethiopia and Seba [to Cyrus] *in exchange for your freedom, as your ransom.* (Is. 43:3 TLB)

Felix Manalo claimed that, since he was sent by God, God would punish those who rejected him (Manalo). If

Dealing With Prospects Who Are of the Iglesia ni Cristo

they reject Manalo, they also reject God. So the Iglesia ni Cristo believed Manalo and obeyed him. Mr. Catabay says:

What is the evil consequence of rejecting those sent by God?

He who hears you hears Me, he who rejects you rejects Me, and he who rejects Me rejects Him who sent Me (Luke 10:16 NKJ).

The verdict is very clear: "...he who rejects you (those who were sent) rejects Me, and he who rejects Me rejects Him (God) who sent Me." To reject the one sent is to reject God who alone has the prerogative and authority to send His messenger. Thus, to accept the one sent is tantamount to accepting God. There is no other way!

How grave is the sin of those who reject God's messenger? It is worse than the sin of Sodom and Gomorrah (*Pasugo* May-June 1986:26).

5. Show the prospect that the verse referred to, Luke 10:16, was Jesus Christ's instructions to the 70 disciples. These were His students who had graduated from their studies. Jesus sent them in twos to win lost souls, so those people might also have everlasting life. When the 70 returned, they gladly reported to Jesus that even the devils obeyed them in Jesus' name. Let the prospect read Luke 10:1,2,16 and 17 with you.

After these things the Lord appointed other seventy also, and sent them two and two before His face into every city and place, whither He Himself would come.

Therefore said He unto them, The harvest truly is great, but the labourers are few: pray ye therefore the Lord of the harvest, that He would send forth labourers into His harvest. (Luke 10:1,2)

He that heareth you heareth Me; and he that despiseth you despiseth Me; and he that despiseth Me despiseth Him that sent Me.

And the seventy returned again with joy, saying Lord, even the devils are subject unto us through Thy name. (Luke 10:16,17)

Felix Manalo claimed to be the "angel ascending from the east." This is how Dr. Sanders described the claim of Manalo:

> In Revelation 7:1,2 reference is made to "Four Angels standing at the four corners of the earth" and to "another angel ascending from the east." Manalo asserts that this fifth angel is to be identified with himself and that the "east" is the Philippines. He points out that the word "angel" is used in two senses, as a heavenly being and as one sent to carry out a mission. He is the angel in the second sense. The "sealing" of the servants means to receive the teaching of Manalo and to believe with one's whole heart. The four angels are Lloyd George, Orlando, Clemenceau, and Wilson who brought to [a] close World War I which is symbolized by the "four winds of the earth" (*Ang Pasugo*, April, 1939).

This is an extravagant and an entirely unsupportable claim (Sanders nd:4) A Protestant View of the Iglesia ni Cristo ("Manalistes").

6. Show the prospect that Felix Manalo was a witness for himself, but the Bible says that one's claim is false when he is a witness for himself. Let the prospect read John 5:31 with you.

If I bear witness of Myself, My witness is not true. (John 5:31)

About Salvation

In the *Pasugo* as quoted by Dr. Gabriel, it states that there is no salvation without acceptance of Manalo.

Ought to accept the last messenger of God; no salvation without acceptance of Manalo (*Pasugo* July 1970, p. 1) (Gabriel 1982:21).

Man's chance for salvation is with the last Messenger (*Pasugo*, Feb. 1972, p. 2) (Gabriel 1982: 22).

The Church of Christ believes that it is the only means of man's salvation in the Christian era.... For man to be saved, he should enter in by Christ, by becoming a member of His Body or Church (John 10:9; 1 Corinthians 12:27; Colossians 1:18). Christ will save His Church (Ephesians 5:23).

Christ will not save anyone outside the Church of Christ because it would be against the law of God. His law requires that sinners should pay for their own sin (Deuteronomy 24:16; Revelation 20:14) (Santiago, *Pasugo* May-June 1986:41).

The Bible does not teach that you must accept Manalo as the messenger of the last days to be saved; nor does it teach that you must enter in the Iglesia ni Cristo or become a member of the same in order to be saved.

1. Show the prospect that all are sinners. No one is righteous, including yourself, the prospect and others. Let him read Romans 3:10 and 23 with you.

As it is written, There is none righteous, no, not one. (Rom 3:10)

For all have sinned, and come short of the glory of God. (Rom. 3:23)

At this point, the prospect might reason that he did not commit any crime.

2. Show the prospect that, according to the Bible, the truth is not in him if he denies committing any crime. Let him read First John 1:8 and 10 with you.

If we say that we have no sin, we deceive ourselves, and the truth is not in us.

If we say that we have not sinned, we make Him a liar, and His word is not in us. (I John 1:8,10)

3. Show the prospect that, as a sinner, he will die. This is the second death, or eternal separation from God. Let him read Romans 6:23 with you.

For the wages of sin is death; but the gift of God is eternal life through Jesus Christ our Lord. (Rom. 6:23)

4. Show the prospect that death means eternal punishment in the lake of fire. Let him read Revelation 21:8 with you.

But the fearful, and unbelieving, and the abominable, and murderers, and whoremongers, and sorcerers, and idolaters, and all liars, shall have their part in the lake which burneth with fire and brimstone: which is the second death. (Rev. 21:8)

5. Show the prospect that God loves all His creatures, that all might have eternal life. Let him read John 3:16 with you.

For God so loved the world, that He gave His only begotten Son, that whosoever believeth in Him should not perish, but have everlasting life. (John 3:16)

6. Show the prospect that if he believes and accepts Jesus Christ as his personal divine Lord and Savior, he is not condemned. But if he does not, he is already condemned. Let him read John 3:18 with you.

He that believeth on Him is not condemned: but he that believeth not is condemned already, because he hath not believed in the name of the only begotten Son of God. (John 3:18)

7. Show the prospect that not all who say, "Lord, Lord" will have everlasting life. Let him read Matthew 7:21 with you.

Not every one that saith unto Me, Lord, Lord, shall enter into the kingdom of heaven; but he that doeth the will of My Father which is in heaven. (Matt. 7:21)

8. Show the prospect that non-believers are children of the devil, satan. Let him read John 8:44 with you.

Ye are of your father the devil, and the lusts of your father ye will do. He was a murderer from the beginning, and abode not in the truth, because there is no truth in him. When he speaketh a lie, he speaketh of his own: for he is a liar, and the father of it. (John 8:44)

At this point, the prospect might be scared and ask you what he needs to do in order to be saved.

Lead Him to Faith in Jesus Christ

Show him the plan of salvation by using Section A of Chapter IX in this book. If he claims to be religious use Section D. If he claims to be righteous, use Section C. If he is not interested in the salvation of his soul, use Section B.

About the Author

The Reverend Doctor Jose A. Lagud has earned four degrees and one honorary degree. He was conferred with a Bachelor of Arts (B.A.) degree and a Bachelor of Science in Education (B.S.E.) degree from Luna Colleges in Tayug, Pangasinan, Philippines. He has a Master of Theology (Th.M.) Magna Cum Laude and a Doctor of Theology (Th.D.) degrees from International Seminary in Plymouth, Florida, as well as a Doctor of Divinity (D.D.), an honorary degree from the same seminary.

After his seminary training, Dr. Lagud has served the Lord God as a pastor of a number of local churches of the United Church of Christ in the Philippines with minimal interruptions, since 1951. In 1961 the Department of Mission of the United Church of Christ in the

Philippines commissioned Dr. Lagud as a missionary and sent him to Hawaii to serve a number of churches there.

In 1978 he organized an evangelical church and became its chairman and senior pastor. It is a conservative church that seeks to preserve the purity of original Christianity and to preserve the purity of the gospel of Jesus Christ, who is our divine Lord and Savior.

Dr. Lagud is married to a devout, born again Christian and an understanding and loving wife: the former Miss Annie Ablog. She was the first Physician of Sindol, San Felipe, Zambales, Philippines. The Lord God has blessed them with two fine children. Joel is 23 and Jo-Ann is 19; they are both studying at the University of Hawaii.

Bibliography

Berkhof, L. *Systematic Theology*. Grand Rapids, Michigan: Eerdman Publishing Company, 1959.

Boa, Kenneth. *World Religion and You*. Wheaton, Illinois: Victor Books, 1980.

Catabay, Tomas C. "The Commission of Brother Felix Manalo". Philippines: *Pasugo* May-June, 1986.

DeHaan, M.R. *Bread for Each Day*. Grand Rapids, Michigan: Radio Bible Class, 1962.

Gabriel, Melanio, Jr. *Ang Mga Lihim at Mga Kabulaanan Ng Iglesia ni Cristo (Manalo)*. Republic of the Philippines: Dr. Melanio Gabriel, Jr., 1982.

Graham, Billy. *The Holy Spirit*. Waco, Texas: A Key-Word Book, Word Books, Publisher, 1978.

Hastings, James. *The Great Text of the Bible*, Volume XI. Grand Rapids, Michigan: Eerdmans Publishing Company, nd.

Larkin, Clarence. *Charts from the Book of Dispensational Truth*. Philadelphia, Pennsylvania: Rev. Clarence Larkin Est. 1920.

Martin, Walter. *Walter Martin's Cults Reference Bible*. Santa Ana, California: Vision House Publishers, 1981.

_____. *The Kingdom of the Cults*. Minneapolis, Minnesota: Bethany House Publisher, 1985.

Manalo, Eranio G. *Pandoctrina*. Quezon City, Philippines: Iglesia ni Cristo, 1980.

Passantino, Robert and Gretchen. *Answers to the Cultist at Your Door*. Eugene, Oregon: Harvest House Publishers, 1981.

Rusthoi, Ralph. *Soul Winning Course*. Montrose, California: Rusthoi Publisher, 1960.

Sanders, Albert J. *The Protestant View of the Iglesia ni Cristo ("Manalista")*. Manila, Philippines: Philippine Federation of Christian Churches, nd.

_____. *Our Protestant Faith*. Manila, Philippines: United Church of Christ in the Philippines, nd.

Santiago, Bienvenido C. *The Belief of the Iglesia ni Cristo*. Philippines: Iglesia ni Cristo, *Pasugo* May-June, 1986.

Schnell, Willian J. *Thirty Years a Watchtower Slave*. Grand Rapids, Michigan: Baker Book House Company, 1971.

Smith, Joseph. *The Book of Mormon*. Salt Lake City, Utah: The Church of Jesus Christ of the Latter Day Saints, 1990.

Stowe, Leland. *Modern Tithing*. Pleasantville, New York: Readers Digest Reprint, 1958:3.4.

Sumner, Robert L. *Falsities of Seventh-Day Adventism!* Murfreesboro, Tennessee: Sword of the Lord Publishers, 1981.

Trauss, Lehman. *The Second Person.* New York: Loizeaux Brothers, 1951.

_____. *The Third Person.* New York: Loizeaux Brothers, 1954.

Tuggy, Arthur Leonard. *The Iglesia ni Cristo.* Quezon City, Philippines: Conservative Baptist Publication Inc., 1976.

Weiss, G. Christian *The Perfect Will of God.* Chicago: Moody Press, 1950.

Webster New World Dictionary. New York and Cleveland, Ohio: The World Publishing Company, 1970.

Wycliffe Bible Commentary. Chicago, Illinois: Moody Press, 1962.

How to Order Additional Copies of This Book

Please complete the order form below and send it with your check or money order to:

>Dr. Jose A. Lagud
>Lagud Christian Ministry
>59-444 Pupukea Road
>Haleiwa, Hawaii, USA 96712

Retail price $7.95 (Proceeds from this endeavor will be used for church planting.)

Order Form

Please send me _____ copies of WITNESSING, SOUL WINNING AND DISCIPLING. Enclosed is a check for the amount of $_____ to cover the cost of the book, plus the cost of shipping and handling and the excise tax.

Retail unit price at $7.95	$_____
Shipping and handling per unit at $2.00	$_____
Excise Tax at .04%	$_____
Total	$_____

Name (print)

_____

Address

_____

City, State & Zip

_____